M000303119

WOMEN
OF THE
WORD

BIBLE
STUDY
SERIES

$\mathcal{L}$OVING

LIKE JESUS

SHARON A. STEELE

Gospel Light

Published by Gospel Light
Ventura, California, U.S.A.
www.gospellight.com
Printed in the U.S.A.

All Scripture quotations, unless otherwise indicated, are taken from the *Holy Bible,*
New International Version®. Copyright © 1973, 1978, 1984 by International Bible
Society. Used by permission of Zondervan Publishing House. All rights reserved.

Other versions used are
KJV—King James Version. Authorized King James Version.
MLB—Modern Language Bible, The New Berkeley Version. Copyright © 1945, 1959, 1969,
1971, 1987, Hendrickson Publishers, Inc. Peabody, MA 01960. Used by permission.
NASB—Scripture taken from the *New American Standard Bible,* © 1960, 1962, 1963, 1968,
1971, 1972, 1973, 1975, 1977, 1995 by The Lockman Foundation. Used by permission.
NEB—From *The New English Bible*. © The Delegates of Oxford University Press and The
Syndics of the Cambridge University Press 1961, 1970, 1989. Reprinted by permission.
NKJV—Scripture taken from the *New King James Version*. Copyright © 1979, 1980, 1982 by
Thomas Nelson, Inc. Used by permission. All rights reserved.
RSV—From the *Revised Standard Version* of the Bible, copyright 1946, 1952, and 1971 by
the Division of Christian Education of the National Council of the Churches of Christ
in the U.S.A. Used by permission.

© 2011 Aglow International. All rights reserved.
Previously published in 1999 in the Aglow Bible Study series as *Loving As Jesus Loves*.

Aglow International is an interdenominational organization of
Christian women and men. Our mission is to lead the lost to Jesus Christ and provide
opportunity for believers to grow in their faith and minister to others.
Our publications are used to help women and men find a personal relationship with
Jesus Christ, to enhance growth in their Christian experience, and to help them
recognize their roles and relationships according to Scripture. For more
information about our organization, please write to Aglow International,
P.O. Box 1749, Edmonds, WA 98020-1749, U.S.A., or call (425) 775-7282.
For ordering or information about the Aglow studies and other
resources, visit the Aglow e-store at www.aglow.org.

Rights for publishing this book outside the U.S.A. or in non-English languages are
administered by Gospel Light Worldwide, an international not-for-profit ministry.
For additional information, please visit www.glww.org, email info@glww.org, or write
to Gospel Light Worldwide, 1957 Eastman Avenue, Ventura, CA 93003, U.S.A.

To order copies of this book and other Gospel Light products in bulk quantities,
please contact us at 1-800-446-7735.

ONTENTS

OREWORD

When the apostle Paul poured out his heart in letters to the young churches in Asia, he was responding to his apostolic call to shepherd those tender flocks. They needed encouragement in their new life in Jesus. They needed solid doctrine. They needed truth from someone who had an intimate relationship with God and with them.

Did Paul know as he was writing that these simple letters would form the bulk of the New Testament? We can be confident that the Holy Spirit did! How like God to use Paul's relationship with these churches to cement His plan and purpose in their lives, and, generations later, in ours.

We in Aglow can relate to Paul's desire to bond those young churches together in the faith. After 1967, when Aglow fellowships began bubbling up across the United States and in other countries, they needed encouragement. They needed to know the fullness of who they were in Christ. They needed relationship. Like Paul, our desire to reach out and nurture from far away birthed a series of Bible studies that have fed thousands since 1973 when our first study, *Genesis*, was published. Our studies share heart to heart, giving Christians new insights about themselves and their relationship with and in God.

In 1998, God's generous nature provided us a rewarding new relationship with Gospel Light. Together we published our Aglow classics as well as a selection of exciting new studies. Gospel Light began as a publishing ministry much in the same way Aglow began publishing Bible studies. Henrietta Mears formed Gospel Light in response to requests from churches across America for the Sunday School materials she had written. Gospel Light remains a strong ministry-minded witness for the gospel around the world.

Our heart's desire is that these studies will continue to kindle the minds of women and men, touch their hearts, and refresh their spirits with the light and life a loving Savior abundantly supplies.

This study, *Loving Like Jesus* by Sharon Steele, will guide you through accepting Jesus' love and learning to extend His love to those people in your life who aren't always easy to love. I know that its contents will richly reward you.

Jane Hansen Hoyt
International President
Aglow International

INTRODUCTION

A new command I give you: Love one another. As I have
loved you, so you must love one another. By this everyone will know
that you are my disciples, if you love one another.

JOHN 13:34-35

Although Jesus has commanded us to love one another, it seems that into everyone's life God sends people who are difficult to love. In addition, we all know people for whom we may have genuine feelings of love, but at times our actions toward them are filled with anger, frustration and impatience. Feelings of love seem to disappear, and we find ourselves battling feelings of disgust, disappointment or even hatred.

God wants His children to become effective, powerful Christians by learning to love with Jesus' love. Often as we attempt to love those who are difficult to love, we find ourselves locked into a fierce battle with Satan. He knows how difficult it is to love those who have hurt us, or even love the people we care about, so he tempts us to be filled with unresolved anger, bitterness and hatred. He knows that as we give in to those natural inclinations, we become ineffective and powerless as children of God.

Fortunately, with God's help, we can learn to love others with Jesus' love. Even when we do not have feelings of love, we can choose to perform the actions of love. The purpose of this study is threefold. Here is what careful examination of Jesus' love and His teachings regarding love can do for you:

1. You can gain a clearer understanding of the true nature of genuine love. Too often the nature of love is misunderstood, and this study will clarify what love is and what love is not.

2. You will be encouraged to fully accept the love of Jesus for you. You cannot genuinely love others until the love of Jesus is active and real in your own life.

3. You will learn how to love even when you don't feel love for others. You will be encouraged to put the practical actions of love into practice. You do not need to wait for feelings of love before you can perform loving actions.

As you understand, accept and practice Jesus' love, you will give the feelings of love an atmosphere in which they can grow and mature. As His love is demonstrated in you, your joy will increase and others will recognize that you are truly His disciple.

An Overview of the Study

This Bible study is divided into four sections:

1. *A Closer Look at the Problem* defines the problem and the goal of the lesson.

2. *A Closer Look at God's Truth* gets you into God's Word. What does God have to say about the problem? How can you begin to apply God's Word as you work through each lesson?

3. *A Closer Look at My Own Heart* will help you clarify and further apply Bible truth in your own life. It will also give guidance as you work toward loving others with the same love Jesus has shown to you.

4. *Action Steps I Can Take Today* is designed to help you concentrate on immediate steps of action.

What You Will Need

• *A Bible*—The main Bible used in this study is the *New International Version,* but you can use whatever Bible translation you are used to reading.

• *A Notebook*—During this study you will want to keep a journal to record what God shows you personally. You may also want to journal additional thoughts or feelings that come up as you go through the lessons. Some questions may require more space than is given in this study book.

• *Time to Meditate*—Give the Holy Spirit time to personalize His Word to your heart so that you can know what your response should be to the knowledge you are gaining.

How to Start and Lead a Small Group

One key to leading a small group is to ask yourself, *What would Jesus do and how would He do it?* Jesus began His earthly ministry with a small group called the disciples, and the fact of His presence made wherever He was a safe place to be. Think of a small group as a safe place. It is a place that reflects God's heart and His hands. The way in which Jesus lived and worked with His disciples is a basic small-group model that we are able to draw both direction and nurture from.

Paul exhorted us to "walk in love, as Christ also has loved us and given Himself for us" (Ephesians 5:2, *NKJV*). We, as His earthly reflections, are privileged to walk in His footsteps, to help bind up the brokenhearted as He did or simply to listen with a compassionate heart. Whether you use this book as a Bible study, or as a focus point for a support group, a church group or a home group, walking in love means that we "bear one another's burdens" (Galatians 6:2, *NKJV*). The loving atmosphere provided by a small group can nourish, sustain and lift us up as nothing else can.

Jesus walked in love and spoke from an honest heart. In His endless well of compassion He never misplaced truth. Rather, He surrounded it with mercy. Those who left His presence felt good about themselves because Jesus used truth to point them in the right direction for their lives. When He spoke about the sinful woman who washed Jesus' feet with her tears and wiped them with her hair, He did not deny her sin. He said, "Her sins, which are many, are forgiven, for she loved much" (Luke 7:47, *NKJV*). That's honesty without condemnation.

Jesus was a model of servant leadership (see Mark 10:43-44). One of the key skills a group leader possesses is the ability to be an encourager of the group's members to grow spiritually. Keeping in personal contact with each member of the group, especially if one is absent, tells each one that he or she is important to the group. Other skills an effective group leader demonstrates include being a good listener, guiding the discussion, as well as guiding the group to deal with any conflicts that arise within it.

Whether you're a veteran or brand new to small-group leadership, virtually every group you lead will be different in personality and dynamic. The constant is the presence of Jesus Christ, and when He is at the group's center, everything else will come together.

OU'RE INVITED!

TO GROW . . .

To develop and reach maturity; thrive; to spring up;
come into existence from a source;

WITH A GROUP . . .

An assemblage of persons gathered or located together;
a number of individuals considered together because of similarities;

TO EXPLORE . . .

To investigate systematically; examine; search into or range over
for the purpose of discovery;

NEW TOPICS

Subject of discussion or conversation.

MEETING

Date _____ Time _____

Place _____

_____

Contact _____

Phone _____

Note: Feel free to fill in and photocopy this as an invitation to hand out or post on your church bulletin board. © 2011 Gospel Light, *Loving Like Jesus*. Permission to photocopy granted.

ℒOVE IS IMPORTANT

Janet attended church every Sunday and faithfully brought her tithes and offerings. She was a gifted musician whose singing had blessed many people. She was an articulate teacher who had a tremendous grasp of God's Word. Regrettably, Janet also had a quick temper and a sharp tongue that could cut a person to shreds in seconds. Although Janet had so much to offer, a lack of love in her actions negated the positive effect of her ministry. Whether Janet didn't recognize the importance of love or just didn't know how to love, her effectiveness for God's kingdom suffered because of it.

A Closer Look at the Problem

Loving is not always easy. We all know people who are difficult to love. Loving actions take time, energy and sometimes money, but in God's sight nothing is more important.

This first chapter will focus on the tremendous importance of expressing God's love. Should you begin to feel discouraged by your own lack of love, don't be tempted to give up. Later chapters will offer practical ways to build love into your own nature. Loving others is God's will for you, and He will give you the strength you need to do it.

As you begin this study, ask God to open your eyes to the importance of love and speak to you through His Word. Ask Him to give you the willingness to apply the truths you discover so that you may grow in your love for others.

A Closer Look at God's Truth

Read Matthew 22:34-40. What question did the expert in the law ask Jesus?

Which is the greatest commandment in the Law?

What was Jesus' answer?

Love the Lord your God with all your heart
and with all your soul and with all your
mind. 'Love Your neighbor as yourself

Why do you think Jesus gave two commands instead of one when the Pharisee asked for the single most important commandment?

Because He thought the 2nd was no different
than the 1st. When we love God fully
We will love our neighbor.

Jesus quoted both of these commands (see Deuteronomy 6:5 and Leviticus 19:18) because both are of vital importance and are related to each other. If we love God, we will honor and obey Him, and He will greatly increase our ability to love others. If we do not love others, it creates a barrier between God and us. How does Jesus relate these two commandments to the Law and the prophets?

all the law and the prophets hang on
these 2 commands in other words
the whole old testament hangs on this

What does Matthew 22:40 mean to you?

That God wants me to love + obey Him.
That I'm to love myself + I'm
to love others. So it was written.

Read Romans 13:8-10. According to this passage, what debt do we always owe to others?

the continuing debt to love one another

What does verse 8 say about the person who loves others?

for he who loves his fellow man
has fulfilled the law

How does obeying the commandment to love fulfill the Law?

All of the Commands in the Law Can be summed up with the direction to love God + to love your neighbor.

If loving is the fulfillment of the Law, what is implied when we do not love?

that we are not obeying God. If we dont obey God, we dont love Him.

When we love God with all of our heart, soul and mind, pleasing Him becomes our priority. As we seek to honor Him through our lives, He increases our desire and our capacity to love others. Love for our neighbors will result in beneficial actions toward them, which means we would never seek to hurt them. Because love is clearly God's commandment to us, the person who is content to live with hatred needs to recognize that he or she is not walking in obedience to God's will.

Read Luke 10:25-28. What question did the expert in the Law ask Jesus?

What must I do to inherit eternal life?

How did Jesus answer him?

What is written in the law? How do you read it?

Why do you think Jesus answered with a question?

B/c the expert already knew the answer

How are we to love God?

With All your heart, with all your soul, with all your strength + with all your mind.

What does it mean to you to love God with all your heart, soul, strength and mind?

that everything that is defined as "you" loves God. He is your complete focus.

The word "heart" refers to the center of one's emotions, even as we today would say someone "broke my heart." "Soul" refers to the inner self or personality, and strength is a reference to one's physical body. The word "mind" refers to the intellect. By putting them all together, the commandment tells us that we are to love God with our entire being. How did He say we are to love others?

We our to love your neighbor as yourself

What does loving your neighbor as yourself involve?

treating others as you would want to be treated. Giving them the same grace that you want yourself.

What was Jesus' response to the expert's answer (see verse 28)?

that the expert answered Correctly and that if he would do it he will live.

How does loving God relate to salvation and trusting in God?

When we are saved we believe Jesus is the Son sent on our behalf by God to save us from our sin. When we have made that eternal decision we are also choosing to obey God. Our obedience shows our love + trust in God.

How does loving others relate to your salvation?

When I have been saved by Jesus + I love God I want others to be saved as well. I should want them to know that same feel of love and trust.

Jesus emphasized that loving God is the most important commandment. It is vital to our salvation. Unless we love God, we can't expect to gain eternal life; and unless we first love and accept Him, we can't love others with His kind of love. Loving God enables us to trust Him and submit to His lordship. As we love Him and accept His lordship over us, He increases our ability to love others. Take a few minutes to evaluate the depth of your love for God. In what ways does your love need to grow?

I need to allow God to assume the position of lordship. I need to let go of wanting to be in control.

According to Luke 10:29-37, what other question did the expert ask Jesus, and what do you think was his motive for asking (see verse 29)?

Who is my neighbor? to justify himself. I think he asked it to trip Jesus up.

How did Jesus answer his question?

he told him a parable + then asked him a question - Which one of these 3 do you think was a neighbor to the man?

Why do you think Jesus answered with a parable, and what did He accomplish with His answer?

The expert had to answer the question honestly

In the parable, why do you think the priest and the Levite went by without stopping? What did their lack of action show?

those are the 2 who should have stopped b/c they were part of the man's community. their lack of action showed no love, compassion or mercy for the man. They didn't want to get involved.

How do their reasons compare to reasons why people today fail to help others?

I think they are the same reasons

What practical demonstrations of love did the Samaritan show?

Bandaged his wounds, gave him his donkey, took him somewhere to be cared for, paid

How did the Samaritan show that he loved his neighbor as himself, and what did it cost him to help?

By caring for him as he would have wanted to be cared for. It cost him, time and money

Why do you think he helped, and what did he gain by helping?

He helped b/c God (HS) moved his heart + he was obedient. A sense a joy and good feeling.

How does this story define a neighbor?

A neighbor is someone you take mercy upon.

In this story, the neighbor was not a person who lived next door. He was not a friend or even an acquaintance. Instead, he was a person in need. The Samaritan proved his love by giving his time, effort and money to help meet that man's need. While we may not often come upon an individual who is physically wounded and bleeding, there are many who are emotionally wounded and bleeding. They desperately need someone to care, and it often takes time and energy to minister to those hurting individuals. It is sad that we are often too busy or too unconcerned to get involved in the lives of those wounded souls in need of someone who cares. Helping others is love in action. Are you willing to give of yourself to reach out to those who are in need? If this is a struggle for you, ask God to give you a willing heart.

Read 1 Corinthians 13:1-3. What gifts of the Holy Spirit are mentioned?

Speak in tongues of men + angels.
gift of prophecy + can fathom all
mysteries + all knowledge
faith to move montins - Generosity

What is the result when a person has these spiritual gifts but lacks love?

Ultimately I gain nothing.
I am spirtually empty.

Why are these gifts so ineffective if not accompanied by love?

B/c the other person knows the gifts
are being given out of a sense of
duty or expectation + they dn't
care the same meaning. They don't
pint people to Jesus.

Why do you think so many people seek certain spiritual gifts rather than trying to build love into their lives?

Its easier - love can be difficult

Although spiritual gifts are desirable, we need to realize that unless they are accompanied by love, their value to us and to Christ's Body will be greatly diminished. Without love, the most impressive manifestation of spiritual gifts, and the noblest sacrifices, mean nothing. We must learn to love, or else these gifts will accomplish little. To be powerful and effective to the kingdom of God, the gifts of the Spirit must be combined with the active love of Jesus in our life. People usually do not care how much we know until they know how much we care.

Read 1 John 2:9-11. What does this passage say about the person who hates?

That he is still in darkness. He does not
know where he is going b/c the
darkness has blinded him

What do these verses tell us about the person who loves?

That they are in the light. Jesus is the light. The person who loves is on the right path

What is promised to the one who loves?

there is nothing in him to make him stumble

What do you think is meant by "the darkness" and "the light"?

light = good, true, holy

darkness - evil + false

Verse 10 is a key to victorious living. Why do you think love is important if we are to live a victorious life in Christ?

B/C when we love we are in the light we are good, true + holy rejecting the darkness seeking Christ

What does verse 10 imply about hatred in our life?

that it blinds us, it keeps us out of the light

In Scripture, darkness usually refers to any area that is under Satan's control. Light refers to an area controlled by God. Love is a characteristic of the light and cannot coexist with the darkness. We need to recognize that if we have an area of hatred in our life, Satan has control of us in that area. This hatred will become a stumbling block, and we won't be able to live victoriously until we allow God to remove it.

A Closer Look at My Own Heart

It is usually no challenge to love kind, lovable people. But how do you love that irritable grouch who consistently rubs you the wrong way? How do you love the one who has taken advantage of you, or who has deeply hurt you or a loved one? When you think of those who are difficult to love, does a specific individual come to mind? As you study the remaining passages, ask God to reveal practical love actions that you can take to begin to build love into those more difficult relationships.

Read Luke 6:27-31. Who does Jesus command us to love in verse 27?

Love your enemies, do good to those who hate you

What actions of love does Jesus ask us to perform (see verses 27-28)?

do good to those who hate you. bless those who curse you pray for those who abuse you.

How do you think obeying these commands would affect your feelings?

It's hard to hold on to the negative feelings when you are doing something kind for someone else

What effect might it have on the other individual?

It might change how they feel about you.

What practical action of love is found in Luke 6:31?

As you wish for others to do to you, do to them.

What are some practical ways that you could apply verse 31 to your relationships?

Speak kind words, Show mercy,
Offer to help in times of need.
Pray

Read Romans 12:17-21. What actions of love are commanded?

Live peaceably with all. if your
enemy is hungry feed him, thirsty
give him a drink. Do not avenge
yourself. Over come evil with good

How do these instructions relate to the actions in Luke 6?

REINFORCES the actions.
Do no evil to others even when its
been done to you - God is in
Charge

What is the main emphasis of these two passages?

Treat others as you want to be
treated - do only good, love others.

When the apostle Paul wrote these instructions, he realized that it might be impossible to live in peace with some people. No matter how hard you try, you cannot force another individual to be at peace with you. Your task is to carefully examine your own actions to honestly determine what you can do to bring peace into the relationship. As you choose to do everything you can to promote peace and perform the actions of love described in these verses, most people will respond favorably to your actions.

In Luke 6:32-36, what actions did Jesus describe that even sinners do?

Love those who love them, lend to sinner
be good to those who are good to them

In what way are Christians to be different in this regard?

We ar to love our enemies + do good + lend w ithout expct anything in return. Be merciful

What will be the results of following Jesus' instructions?

We are being obedient to God. God will have mercy on us.

What do these verses show us about God's love?

That it is complete - He loves us all the time

The principles found in these passages from Luke and Romans are among the most powerful in Scripture in teaching us how to love those who are difficult to love. These Scriptures are not intended to teach us to become doormats for other people. Instead they teach us the principle of overcoming evil by doing good.

A story is told of a young soldier who, because of his strong Christian beliefs, was teased unmercifully by those in his barracks. Yet every night the young man knelt by his bed to pray. One night, an especially tough sergeant picked up his dirty boots and threw them at the young praying soldier, hitting him in the head. Everyone laughed, but the young man continued to pray. The next morning, the sergeant found his boots, cleaned and shined, beside his bed. He was so touched by the soldier's reaction that it broke through his tough shell and he gave his life to the Lord that day. The soldier had done what he could to promote peace.

Satan wants you to be full of anger and bitterness. When others mistreat you or your loved ones, it is natural to want to retaliate, but retaliation increases feelings of animosity. However, if you will choose to do good to those who hurt you, blessing and praying for them, those feelings of anger and hatred will begin to dissipate. Love is one of God's most powerful weapons against the forces of Satan.

You can't always control your thoughts and feelings, but you can, by an act of the will, choose to respond to those feelings with God's love. If you will choose to pray every time you have a bitter or hateful thought toward another person, those feelings will lose their power to control you. Ask God to show you any actions of love that you can perform to help meet that person's need. If you do what He tells you, you will be amazed at the change in your feelings. God will be honored and glorified as you show His kind of love.

Action Steps I Can Take Today

Evaluate the depth of your love for God. In your journal, honestly describe your love relationship with the Lord. Ask God to reveal to you any areas in which you have been loving Him with halfhearted devotion. Then write a prayer asking Him for strength to make any needed changes.

As you honestly evaluate the depth of your love toward others, you might want to ask yourself the following questions:

- *Am I too busy or too unconcerned to help those in need?*
- *To whom can I show God's love in a tangible way today?*
- *Is a lack of love hindering my effectiveness as a Christian?*
- *Is hatred for anyone destroying my walk with God? (If yes, will you confess that hatred as sin and ask God to help you get rid of it?)*

Choose actions of love. *Ask God to show you those people to whom you need to show genuine love.* Write a prayer in your journal asking God to teach you how to love with His love.

Ask God for specific ways to pray for those who need your love. Record the ways you've prayed so that you will not forget them.

Ask God for creative ways to demonstrate love. Make a list in your journal of all the ideas He brings to your mind. Determine that, with God's help, you will begin to put those actions into practice. Record any actions taken and the results of your actions.

TWO

LOVE IS POWERFUL

Mary walked into the church not knowing what to expect. A close friend had invited her, and she had, somewhat reluctantly, agreed to go. Throughout the worship service, she kept sensing that there was something wonderfully different about these people. They were so warm and seemed to genuinely care about each other. As the service came to a close, Mary felt overwhelmed with emotion and began to cry. When her friend asked her what was wrong, she replied, "I want what they have."

Mary had been so touched by God's love flowing through His people that she accepted Jesus as her Savior that very night. Love's incredible power had drawn her to the one who is the ultimate source of love.

A Closer Look at the Problem

It is easy to see that God has commanded us to love, and that our love or lack of love for others can be a reflection of our relationship with Him. Unfortunately, just knowing those things does not necessarily make us more loving. Sometimes it is extremely difficult to love another person, and our lack of love can leave us with staggering feelings of guilt and failure. We need more than just to know that we should love. We need an unfailing source of love who can enable us to love when our human ability to love is not enough. The dual focus of this chapter is to realize and appreciate these truths:

1. Love is an incredible power.
2. God is your ultimate source of love, and His power will enable you to love when you simply cannot love through your own strength.

Before you open God's Word, ask Him to speak to you as you read it and help you apply what you learn to your life and your relationships.

A Closer Look at God's Truth

LOVE'S AWESOME POWER

Read Colossians 2:2-3. What was Paul's twofold intention for ministry to these people?

Encouraged in heart + united in love

What did he hope would be the result of the encouragement and unity?

that they might know Christ

What result of love is found in Colossians 3:14?

binds them all together in perfect unity

What role do you think love plays in uniting people? Why?

love helps you accept other people even when they are different + when you love people you are making the decision to be on the same page.

Love is God's most powerful force for unifying His people. His love enables us to accept others, including their faults. This unconditional acceptance is essential to unity. What result of love is mentioned in John 13:34-35? Why do you think this result occurs?

Everyone will know that you are a disciple of Jesus

What is the result in the world when Christians don't love each other?

Chaos. People don't care for one another. Poverty, hatred

Without Jesus' love, none of us has the capacity to love the unlovable or love those who have hurt us. When we reach out in love to hard-to-love people, the world will recognize that we are different. This difference will identify us as belonging to Jesus, because we are following His example of love. In John 17:20-23, which phrase indicates that you are included in Jesus' prayer?

those who believe in Jesus through the message heard from other believers

What are the phrases from Jesus' prayer that suggest Christians are to be united and loving toward each other?

If Christians are united others will believe

- We are one -

What are the results of loving unity between Christians?

Others coming to know Jesus.

Why does love for each other have such an impact upon unbelievers?

B/c it shows them we are different. We have something they can have if they choose to.

Love is one of God's most powerful magnets to draw us to Himself. People desperately want and need to love and to be loved. When people of the world see Jesus' love and acceptance among believers, they will be drawn to Him. Our love for each other is proof to the world that Jesus came and that He loves *all* of us. Trying to shame or condemn people into a right relationship with God usually drives them further away. Honest, caring love, as demonstrated through the life of Jesus, is God's power to draw people to Himself.

What tragic result of division is described in Luke 11:17?

the Kingdom will be ruined - + a house divided will fail

How does this apply to a home? How does this apply to a fellowship?

Home - no unity - discord ⎫
Fellowship - no closeness ⎭ Loss of intimacy

Love has the power to unite, and it is only through love that a home or a church body can be built up and strengthened. Fighting, bickering and a lack of love show that God's Spirit is not in control. From 1 John 3:16-20; 4:19-21, list all the phrases that suggest the results of loving one another.

lay down our lives for our brothers + sisters, Give to others in need, have compassion, we must love our brother + sister

What do you think is meant by 1 John 3:17 (see also James 2:14-17)?

We are to share our possessions with those in need

How do our words express love?

When we speak kindly, express appreciation, thankfulness.

Why will actions of love set our hearts at rest in God's presence?

B/c those actions are actually towards God. It's an expression of worship for Him

How can love drive out fear?

Love is the ultimate realization that God loves us. If He is for us who can be against us.

It is important to realize that words of love are not being condemned in these verses. People need to hear our expressions of love. There are times, however, when words alone are not enough. When a person has a physical, spiritual or emotional need that we can help meet, true love will express itself by helping to answer that need.

When we perform actions of love, one result is a sense of assurance that we belong to God. Sometimes our hearts condemn us and make us feel guilty even when God hasn't condemned us. Revelation 12:10 tells us that Satan is the accuser of Christians, and he delights in a guilt-ridden, defeated child of God. One way in which we can receive peace and assurance of salvation is through actions of love toward others.

What is promised in 1 John 3:21-24?

If we keep His commands & obey him we will receive from Him what we ask — Spirit of God lives in us

What commands must we obey to receive these promises?

to believe in his Son, Jesus, to love one another

How does love or lack of love affect one's prayer life?

lack of love drives us from prayer. When we feel love we will pray

How do obedience and faith affect one's prayers?

Deeper, more meaningful. full of faith

Love is a condition to having our prayers answered (see 1 John 3:21-23). We must believe in Jesus and love one another. If we have love in our hearts for others, we are more likely to feel confident in approaching God. If we're experiencing hatred, it is extremely difficult to draw into God's presence. Faith and obedience are also important. Without faith, we limit God's power in our lives (see Matthew 13:58). If we are deliberately disobedient, we feel ashamed to draw into His presence, and our prayer life is severely hindered.

Take a few minutes to reflect on your prayer life. In your journal, describe how these verses apply to you and to your prayer life. List any changes you need to make before you can have power in prayer. Write a prayer asking God to help you make those changes.

LOVE'S ULTIMATE SOURCE

Annette recognized the importance of love and knew she *should* love. Unfortunately, she also knew her heart and felt overwhelmed by the ugliness of her feelings. Unresolved anger, bitterness, hatred and doubt left her with such staggering feelings of guilt and failure she hesitated to draw into God's presence. Why would God bother to answer such a pathetic failure?

Annette had fallen prey to one of Satan's cleverest deceptions. She felt too ashamed to go to God, yet He was the *only one* able to clean her up and enable her to love. A mature Christian friend prayed with Annette that she would recognize how precious she was to God, and He powerfully answered that prayer. Annette learned to walk in God's grace. As she experienced a new awareness of God's love toward her, she was able to draw into His presence and receive His power to love.

As you look at the following passages, ask God to show you how you can more fully connect with Him to receive His power to love.

According to 1 John 4:7-8,16, who is the source of love?

God

God is love

How is God described in verses 8 and 16?

God is Love

In these verses, the Greek words that are translated as "love" are either *agape* (noun form) or *agapeo* (verb form). Both describe a benevolent, self-giving love that always seeks the highest good for the other individual. What does verse 7 tell us about the person who "has been born of God"?

EVERYONE WHO LOVES # has been born of God, KNOWS God

What does it mean to be born of God?

Accepted Jesus — Loves God + acknowledge God loves US.

It is important to realize that God's very nature is self-giving love and that He is the ultimate source of love. When we receive Jesus as Savior and Lord of our lives, we are born of God's Spirit, and God's love becomes active within us. At that moment, His Spirit indwells us and begins the renewing process. It is His Spirit within us that empowers us to love others and gives us a desire to reach out to them.

Read Galatians 5:13-26. What instruction about love is given in verse 13?

Serve one another humbly - loving one another makes us free

What does verse 14 teach about love?

the entire law is fulfilled by loving your neighbor as yourself.

What actions are we warned against in verse 15, and why?

If you bite + devour each other you will destroy one another

What does "biting and devouring each other" mean?

fighting - talking against one another discord.

What is the struggle between the sinful nature and the spiritual nature (see verses 17-26)?

our nature is contrary to that of God we are not to do whatever we want

How can we overcome the downward pull of the sinful nature?

Keep in step with the Spirit - do not be conceited, don't provoke others, do not envy others

Describe what you think is meant by the phrase "live by the Spirit" (verse 25)?

STAY close to God, Pray, Worship -
follow Gods commands

List the acts of the sinful nature (see verses 19-21). Which show a lack of love?

Sexual immorality, impunty, debauchery,
idolatry + witchraft, hatred, discord,
jealousy, fits of rage, Selfish ambition, dissensions,
envy, drunkeness orgies, factions

What are the fruit of the Spirit found in Galatians 5:22-23?

love, joy, peace, forbearance, kindness
goodness, faithfulness, gentleness +
Self Control

It is important to recognize that the sinful nature is always present in our lives and that it is in conflict with the spiritual nature. It is a natural tendency of the flesh to respond to hurtful situations with hatred, discord and fits of rage. Without the power of God's Spirit, we cannot respond with love. We cannot overcome these natural tendencies toward sin in our own strength. It is only when we live by the power of God's Spirit that we are able to gain victory over them.

A Closer Look at My Own Heart

Take a few moments to consider your own heart condition, asking God to show you any of the acts of the sinful nature that may be present in your life. Confess them as sin and ask God to cleanse you.

The key to overcoming the acts of the sinful nature is to live by God's Spirit. As you do, His love within you begins to produce the fruit of the Spirit to replace the acts of the sinful nature. As you draw closer and closer to Him, the fruit of the Spirit will become more and more evident in your life.

As you read John 15:1-12, list all phrases that show the futility of trying to bear spiritual fruit through human strength and effort.

No branch can bear fruit by itself, it must remain on
the vine. Apart from me you can do nothing

What does it mean to "remain," or abide, in Jesus?

Stay close - allow the Holy Spirit to lead

What is promised to the one who remains or abides in Jesus?

ask whatever you wish & it will be done for you - to God's glory

What are the results of not remaining in Jesus (see verses 4-6)?

a branch that withers or is thrown into the fire + burned

What is each person's responsibility?

to keep God's commands

How does this passage relate to the fruit of the Spirit?

The fruit of the Spirit comes from God. If we remain in Him we will bear fruit

It is essential that you recognize that God is the ultimate source of love and that love is a fruit of God's Holy Spirit. It is only through remaining closely connected to Jesus that you are able to bear the fruit of God's Spirit. When His Spirit fills and controls your life, the natural result is love toward others and a growth within you of the fruit of the Spirit.

Although God is the one who produces the fruit of the Spirit, there is also an element of human responsibility. You cannot expect to grow in the Spirit unless you are intimately connected to God. You must also feed your spiritual nature through frequent worship, prayer and Bible study. Neither can you expect to grow if you are in willful disobedience to God. Remaining or abiding in Jesus implies a day-to-day, minute-by-minute relationship with Him. Without that close relationship, your life will not produce the fruit of the Spirit.

What result of the Spirit-filled life is described in Romans 5:5?

We will have hope

How do the truths in 2 Corinthians 3:17-18 relate to our ability to love?

when we have the spirt of the lord we are free to love as we love we are transformed into the image of God+ this allows us to love more

Summarize what Matthew 26:41, Ephesians 3:16-21 and 1 Peter 2:2 say about living a victorious, fruitful life in the Spirit.

Watch + pray; Stay connected in the Church + to God's people - allow the Holy Spirit to lead. Crave to learn

What is an area of your spiritual life in which you need to grow?

Crave to learn, pray, let the Holy Spirit lead

Which promise is most meaningful to you? What condition is given as a requirement for fulfilling that promise?

Watch + pray

Through God's Holy Spirit, you have power to enable you to live a fruitful, effective life filled with His kind of love. Attempting to love in your own strength will only lead to frustration and failure. You must lay hold of God's power by being continuously filled with His Spirit. It is only by the power of God's Spirit that the fruit of the Spirit can be reproduced in you.

Many people experience a dramatic filling of the Holy Spirit. Following that experience, they see much evidence of the fruit of the Spirit in their lives. Tragically, many expect that one experience to carry them on a spiritual high indefinitely. They don't feed the spiritual nature and make no effort to grow in the Spirit. The result is spiritual disaster. They are weak and ineffective; they have no joy in the Lord and no victory. They live as defeated Christians. Unfortunately, they often bring dishonor to the name of Jesus and to the reputation of the Holy Spirit.

You cannot expect a one-time experience to empower you for life. In Ephesians 5:18, Paul commands you to be filled with the Spirit. The Greek word that is used for "filled" is in the continuous present tense, which implies that you are to be filled with God's Spirit *now,* and you are to *continuously* be filled. You need to seek God daily and ask for His continuous filling and empowering. It is only as you draw near to God and let His Spirit continually fill and control you that you are able to love those who are difficult to love. If it is your desire to grow in your ability to love, strengthen your relationship with God. Keep on being filled with the Spirit.

Action Steps I Can Take Today

Evaluate the power of love in your life. In your journal, write an honest assessment of how God's love in you is affecting others. Ask God to show you areas where you need to improve, and then write a prayer asking Him for His strength to improve in those areas.

Evaluate your life in regard to the acts of the sinful nature Paul lists in Galatians 5:19-21. Review the acts of the sinful nature, asking God to reveal areas where the sinful nature may be in control of your life.

Evaluate your life in regard to the fruit of the Spirit. Review the fruit of the Spirit listed in Galatians 5:22-23 and identify which fruit is most evident in your life. Which is least evident? Ask God to show you practical ways in which you can remain more closely connected to the life-changing power of His Spirit. Write in your journal any ideas that come to mind.

Choose steps to strengthen your walk with God. Ask God to show you any areas of disobedience that are hindering the work of God's Spirit in your life. Record in your journal any areas God reveals to you.

As God reveals areas of disobedience, choose to confess those as sin and turn away from them.

Ask God to fill you with His Holy Spirit today, and in faith believe that He will. Seek the continuous filling of His Spirit.

Make time spent with God a priority in your life. List the steps you need to take to do this.

If you are struggling with loving another individual, ask God to empower you to love that person through His Spirit in you.

THREE

LOVE IS ACCEPTING

Susan was young when she married, but she was careful to marry a believer. Her mother, who was married to an unbeliever, had often told her, "If you marry a Christian, you won't have the problems that your dad and I have had." Susan married, fully expecting to have no problems. She knew that her new husband would always be gentle and unselfish, eager to please her, and would instinctively understand and meet her emotional needs. He would be a wise, wonderful husband and father, and together they would most certainly live "happily ever after."

Unfortunately, her husband had faults and didn't seem to have the vaguest idea of how to meet her emotional needs. What Susan did not realize was that no man could have lived up to her expectations. His faults and her unmet needs became her focus. Sabotaged by unrealistic expectations and a focus on the negative, the love Susan had once felt disappeared. In place of love, Susan now harbored a critical spirit and experienced great disappointment. As she struggled in the relationship with her husband, it became more and more difficult to draw close to God. Ashamed of her feelings, she doubted that God could still love and accept her.

A Closer Look at the Problem

No human being is perfect. We all have faults. A wise person remarked, "You won't have a perfect marriage because you're married to a sinner. And what makes it even worse is that your spouse is married to one, too!" Often we come into a relationship with unrealistic expectations. People disappoint us and fail to live up to our standards. How can we love them in spite of our unmet needs and disappointments?

Beginning with this lesson, each of the remaining chapters will examine specific actions of Jesus' love toward us. You will see how you can build these same actions of love into your life whether you have *feelings* of love or not. This chapter will demonstrate that acceptance is both an action and an attribute of love. Here is the dual focus of this lesson:

1. To recognize how the love of Jesus reaches out to accept you, even with your faults and weaknesses. You will be encouraged to fully receive His accepting love for you.

2. To learn practical ways to overcome a negative focus and build accepting love into your relationships.

Before you begin the study of God's Word, ask Him to open the eyes of your heart to receive His truth and give you a willingness to apply what you learn.

A Closer Look at God's Truth

A New Command

In John 13:34-35, how did Jesus command His disciples to love?

As Jesus had loved them, they were to love one another

What would be the result of that kind of love?

Freedom, Acceptance

Why do you think Jesus called this a *new* commandment, as Leviticus 19:18 also commands, "love your neighbor as yourself"?

You are now to love others as Jesus loved them - not as you love yourself.

Although the Old Testament does command us to love our neighbor, these verses from John 13 present a new standard of love. We are now given the command to love others as Jesus loved us. What words or phrases would you use to describe the love of Jesus?

Unconditional, open, Accepting,

THE ACCEPTING LOVE OF JESUS

According to Romans 5:8, how is the love of God demonstrated?

Christ died for us .

What phrase implies that Jesus' love is accepting?

We were sinners.

What do John 3:16-17 and 1 John 3:1 tell about God's love and acceptance?

that He loves the world - He wants everyone to
come to Him
We are His children

How is God described in Ephesians 2:4-9?

Rich in mercy

What does God's love do for us?

Saves us. We will be in Heaven w/God

According to Luke 15:11-24, what were the actions of the younger son that would make it difficult for the father to accept him?

he demanded his inheritance, he left &
lived a wild life

Why did he decide to return to his father?

He was broke, everyone had left him, he realized being a servant in his fathers house would be better than what he was doing

What emotions do you think the son felt as he drew close to home?

Shame, fear, uncertainty, apprehension

How do you think he felt as he saw his father running toward him?

A little fearful — possibly happy

How did the father demonstrate his loving acceptance of his son even before the son asked for forgiveness? How did the father show that he accepted him _as a son?_

ran to him, hugged + Kissed him. called for his servants to bring robe, ring sandals + kill fatted calf.

In Luke 15:25-32, how did the older brother react to his brother's return?

Angry, resentful

What was his focus?

On himself + all he had done + how he felt cheated

What do you think would have happened to the younger brother if the father had acted the way the older brother did?

No reconciliation – younger brother might have been lost forever.

What effect did the older brother's lack of acceptance have on the father?

None – He told the older son was always with him + everything he had was his but they had to celebrate.

How was the older brother's attitude affected by his unwillingness to accept his brother?

It made him more resentful, bitter. Took his focus off what was truly important

What does this parable show about the love of God?

God loves us even when we turn our back or when we rail against him.

The accepting and forgiving love of God is beautifully portrayed in this parable. The younger son had made a real mess of his life and had undoubtedly caused his father much grief and sorrow. Yet the father did not look at his own hurts. The father saw his son returning, and with great love he *ran* to meet his son where he was. Although the son asked to be received as a servant, the father called for the finest robe, a ring for his finger and sandals for his feet to be brought *quickly*. His accepting love did not want his son to grovel, even for a minute. The robe, the ring and the sandals clearly identified the young man, not as a servant, but as a beloved son. Then the father shared his great joy by holding a big welcome-home party.

This parable portrays not only the accepting love of God, but also the quality of *agape* love that seeks the highest good for the other individual. While the father's heart must have longed for his son, he did not send help to the distant country, which would have enabled the son to stay there. His love allowed the son to experience the consequences of his own actions. These consequences were a key factor in the son's return home.

This is how God's love reaches out to us. He will allow us to make a mess of our lives and experience the circumstances that come as a result. The painful consequences are allowed to draw us back to Himself. Then when God sees a repentant heart, He meets us right where we are. He doesn't wait for us to be mature and holy before His accepting love reaches out to receive us. He quickly accepts repentant sinners as His children; and because of His love, mercy and grace, He clothes us with His robes of righteousness.

GOD'S ACCEPTING LOVE TOUCHES YOU

Take a few moments to carefully examine your own heart. Perhaps you feel that you have made a mess of your life. Do you realize that God's love eagerly receives repentant sinners and will quickly accept you, even with your failures and shortcomings? His love longs to receive you into intimate fellowship as His own precious child. Write a paragraph thanking God for His love that sees beyond your faults and joyfully accepts you as His beloved child.

_____

_____

_____

_____

_____

_____

If you have difficulty fully believing that God's love will accept you, ask a trusted Christian friend to pray with you in this regard. It will be difficult for you to reach out in love to another unless you first feel the acceptance of God toward you. His love will eagerly accept you, and He longs to draw you into His arms of love just as the father in this story loved and embraced his wayward son.

How do you relate to a prodigal? Perhaps you know someone who is making a real mess of his or her life. Consider the following questions:

- Are your actions in any way enabling the person to continue in sin? If yes, ask God to show you ways that your love can be a healthy love that will help to bring that sinner to repentance.

- Do your actions toward that individual more closely resemble the actions of the father in the parable or the actions of the older son?

Ask God to show you ways that you can show loving acceptance while not enabling the person to continue in sin. Write down any ideas He gives you.

_____

_____

_____

_____

REACHING OUT WITH LOVING ACCEPTANCE TO OTHERS

In Romans 14:1-12, what are we commanded to do in verse 1?

Accept others without quarreling over disputable matters

_____

Why are we commanded to accept others without judgment?

Because God has accepted us as we are - who are we to judge?

_____

What do verses 9-12 teach us about judging? Why were these people judging each other (see verse 5)?

Why judge? We will all stand before God's judgment seat. We judge b/c we believe ours is the "right" way

These people had a difference of opinion. Some, having come from a strong Jewish background, held certain days as sacred occasions, but these days held no special significance to the Gentile believers. There was also a question of whether the meat found in the markets had come from animals that had been used in sacrifice to pagan gods. As a result, some refrained from eating meat altogether. Others believed that since pagan gods had no power, there was no harm in eating the meat and enjoying it. They thanked God for it. Both of these groups had chosen actions they felt would honor God, and both were convinced they had chosen correctly.

Paul emphasized that because both groups had chosen their actions in honor to God, He had accepted the actions of both. A problem arose when one group did not accept the other. Instead, they judged each other, not because their actions were wrong, but because they were different.

What are some issues today that might be similar to the questions of special days and unclean food as shown in this passage?

drinking, dancing, Sundays.

According to Romans 14:13-23, what attitudes do we need to demonstrate toward persons whose actions are different from ours (see verse 13)?

do not put a stumbling block or obstacle in anothers path. acceptance, tolerance

How does verse 15 relate to the instructions in the second part of verse 13?

this may become a stumbling block or obstacle for that person to believe

What important action of love is described in verses 15, 20 and 21?

What you choose to eat + drink

What are some ways an individual's actions can destroy the work of God?

if your actions are a reflection of what you want + not to honor God

What are we commanded to do in verse 19?

Make every effort to do what leads to peace + mutual edification

What are some practical actions you could take that lead to peace and
building others up?

*Speak kindly to one another. Choosing
to say nothing when you disagree*

What is the proper relationship between freedom in Christ and love for
each other?

*We must believe in Christ, Obey Him
Then we will have freedom which
will allow us to love one
another*

In these verses, Paul warned the Roman believers against judging God's
servants. Just as you would not go into another person's business and begin to correct his employees, God doesn't want us judging or condemning
His servants. That's neither our business nor our calling. At the same time,
Paul urged that we conduct ourselves in such a manner that we will not
cause others to stumble. If what we are doing in the exercise of our freedom
in Christ causes another to stumble in his or her walk with the Lord, we are
not acting out of love. We might need to limit our freedom to help another Christian who is weaker (who feels more restricted in what is appropriate Christian behavior).

In Romans 15:1-7, what actions of love are described in verses 1 and 2?

*Bear the failings of the weak.
Build them up*

How do the Scriptures help us during difficult times in our relationships
with others (see verse 4)?

*Shows how people endured & were
encouraged*

What key to unity is found in verse 5, and how would this build unity?

*having the same attitude of mind
toward each other that Jesus
had*

What does verse 7 command us to do, and what will be the result?

Accept one another - This brings praise to God.

What does it mean to you to "accept one another . . . as Christ accepted you"?

That we accept others differences their flaws, acknowledge they are sinners + yet still love them

Why do you think accepting one another will bring praise to Jesus?

The result of acceptance is peace - When we obey Jesus others see the difference + know Jesus is the cause

Accepting the weaknesses of others is not common to human nature. Our human nature wants others to change to fit our standards before we will accept them. Our natural tendency is to be critical and judgmental. Jesus, however, did not come into the world to condemn it (see John 3:17), and we are called to follow His example. A critical, condemning attitude pushes people away from us and from God. Accepting others with their faults will help to draw them to Jesus, allowing Him to change them. Following Jesus and gaining encouragement and hope from the Scriptures will help us accept others in spite of their weaknesses.

A Closer Look at My Own Heart

Take a few minutes to carefully examine your own heart regarding your ability to accept others. What characteristics do you find hardest to accept in others?

_____

_____

_____

_____

_____

Read Luke 6:37-45. As you read this passage, let God reveal truth to you regarding any judgmental tendencies in you. In the chart below, list the phrases in verses 37 and 38 that describe specific actions. What is the expected result of each action?

Action	Result
if you judge	you will be judged
if you condemn	you will be condemned
forgive	forgiven
give	given to you

What do verses 41 and 42 teach about condemning?

When we condemn others we are ignoring our own sin.

What do you think is meant by the statement, "For with the measure you use, it will be measured to you" (verse 38)?

You can expect from others what you give to others

How does that statement relate to love and acceptance?

If you show people love + acceptance they will show you love + acceptance

How does it relate to judgment and condemnation?

Same. If you are judging + condemning they will do the same to you.

We all want to be loved and accepted by others. It is important to realize that it is only as we love and accept others that they will love and accept us in return. If we are critical, condemning people, others will be critical and condemning of us. If we are loving and accepting, we are usually loved and accepted in return. What important truth concerning our words and actions is found in Luke 6:45?

The words that came out of our mouth show the attitude of our heart

Although we want to respect people, it is impossible to truly accept others until we change our way of thinking. We often come into relationships with unrealistic expectations. Instead of viewing people as sinners with shortcomings and faults just like ours, we somehow expect them to never fail us. When they do, we tend to make mental lists of the ways we have been hurt or disappointed. As we focus on their failures, our lists of grievances increase in magnitude and importance. Then, because we want to be loving, we try to speak or act with love and acceptance while still clinging to our hurts or disappointments. Unfortunately, it doesn't work. We fool no one. A person usually knows when you accept and respect him or her and can tell if you are insincere.

The only way you can treat a person with genuine respect and acceptance is to *change your way of thinking* about that individual. First, you need to give up unrealistic expectations. Then you need to ask God to show you how He sees that person and show you his or her good qualities. You can take note of those qualities and daily thank God for those good attributes. You can also begin to show appreciation to the person for his or her commendable qualities.

As you change your focus from the failures to the good qualities, you often find sincere feelings of respect and acceptance growing within you. Your actions toward that person will begin to demonstrate loving acceptance. As your actions and attitudes change, the other individual will usually sense that change and feel free to grow and develop additional positive qualities.

Sometimes your expectations of yourself are even more unrealistic than your expectations of others. You dislike yourself because you can't live up to your own expectations. As you focus on your negative qualities,

Satan gains more power to control you. Ask God to show you your positive qualities and begin to focus on strengthening them. God will build you up; and as you mature, your good qualities will increase.

According to Philippians 4:8, what should be the focus of your mind?

Whatever is true, noble, right,
pure lovely, Admirable, excellent
& praise worthy

Ask God to help you change the focus of your mind to the good.

Action Steps I Can Take Today

Prayerfully ask God to show you your heart. Write in your journal any insights He gives you. Ask God to help you honestly answer the following questions:

- In what ways am I treating others with acceptance?
- In what ways am I judging or condemning others?

Ask God to show you how He views the person you are having difficulty accepting. Ask God to reveal to you that person's good qualities and any areas where he or she may be hurting. Record in your journal what God reveals to you about that individual.

Thank God every day for the good in that person, and ask God to meet his or her needs. This will help you overcome any negative focus.

Memorize and personalize Philippians 4:8. Write it on a card and place the card where you can frequently be reminded of those things you need to focus on. Daily choose to focus on that which is good.

Finally, brothers and sisters, Whatever is true, Whatever is noble, Whatever is right, Whatever is pure, Whatever is lovely, Whatever is admirable - If anything is excellent or praiseworthy - think about such things.

$\mathscr{L}$OVE IS FORGIVING

Nothing within Marie desired to forgive. The pain of an abusive childhood had taken its toll. She felt abandoned, abused, hurt and extremely angry. Fearing that forgiveness would only open the door for more hurt, she fiercely hung on to her grievances. Her unresolved anger and feelings of unforgiveness eventually turned to bitter cynicism against people in general. She had difficulty relating in a positive way to anyone. Marie's anger at her parents turned into anger at God. Why had He allowed such abuse, and why did the abuse continue to devastate her life so many years later? It seemed that the childhood abuse had destined her to a lifetime of misery.

A Closer Look at the Problem

We live in a world that is cursed by sin. As a result, some people seem to be deliberately abusive. Others, through their careless or thoughtless actions, can hurt our feelings, disappoint us and leave us wounded. The natural human tendency is to refuse to forgive the offending individual. Unfortunately, unforgiveness and unresolved anger only prolong pain, prevent healing and sabotage future relationships.

This chapter will show you that Jesus' love toward us is a forgiving love. If we are to love as Jesus loves us, we must also extend forgiveness to others. Here is the threefold focus of this lesson:

1. To help you fully receive God's forgiveness.
2. To show you how unresolved anger hinders forgiveness, and illustrate practical steps to overcome that obstacle.
3. To teach you how to extend forgiveness toward others, even when you do not want to.

Before you begin your study, ask God to show you any areas of unforgiveness or unresolved anger in your life. Ask Him to help you apply the truths of His Word to your relationships.

A Closer Look at God's Truth

THE FORGIVING LOVE OF JESUS

In Matthew 9:1-8, why do you think Jesus addressed the man's need for forgiveness before He healed him?

B/c the man needed to know he was forgiven so he could leave past behind & truly be healed

What does verse 6 teach about Jesus and forgiveness?

that Jesus had the authority to forgive sin

What did the man's healing demonstrate?

His Faith in Jesus / God

Though the religious leaders questioned Jesus' right to forgive, this passage clearly demonstrates both His willingness and His divine authority to do so. According to John 8:3-11, in what sin had this woman become entangled, and what punishment did the law prescribe for that sin?

Adultery - Stone her

What standard for condemning others did Jesus express in verse 7?

let anyone without sin be the first to throw a stone at her

Why do you think the oldest of the accusers left first?

They understood what Jesus said to them.

What does verse 11 teach us about Jesus' forgiveness?

Jesus does not condemn us. He offers forgiveness + expects obedience

The sad truth is that all of us sin and are in need of Jesus' forgiveness. It is easy to look at the sin of others and feel smug or self-righteous. Jesus asked these accusers to examine themselves; as they did so, they saw their own sin. It is interesting that the older individuals were more quickly aware of the sin in their lives than the younger ones.

Jesus wants us to examine ourselves. As we become aware of our own sin, we are not so quick to condemn others. His love reaches out to the worst of sinners, and He stands ready and willing to forgive. Then He asks that we leave our lives of sin, and He empowers us to change.

Read Matthew 26:67-68 and 27:26-31. List the ways Jesus was mistreated.

Spit in his face, Struck + slapped him, Jesus was flogged, Put crown of thorns on him, Stripped him, Mocked him, Crucified him

According to Luke 23:32-34, how did Jesus react to the mistreatment He received?

Asked God to forgive the people who were mistreating Him.

Why was Jesus able to respond the way He did?

He was without sin. He's faith

What effect do you think His forgiveness might have had on those who had mistreated Him?

They might have felt ashamed of their behavior, repentant

In some mysterious way, the act of forgiveness seems to release the power of God to work in another's life. Notice that less than two months after Jesus had asked God to forgive those who had mistreated Him, 3,000 people were saved in one day (see Acts 2:41). Possibly many of those 3,000 were the same individuals who had been in Jerusalem screaming for Jesus' crucifixion. They had mocked Him, spit on Him and watched as He was crucified, but He asked God to forgive them. Love means forgiving; Jesus was able to respond to cruel mistreatment with the forgiveness that comes from unselfish love. His love, which manifested itself in forgiveness, had a life-changing effect on those for whom He prayed.

It is often difficult to forgive those who have hurt you. It is sometimes even harder to forgive those who have hurt the people you love. One way that you can develop a forgiving spirit is to choose to pray for that person who has caused the pain, just as Jesus prayed for those who were hurting Him. When you pray for the person who has hurt you or those you love, forgiveness begins to grow within you. The anger loses its power and the hurts begin to heal as you pray for the offender.

What does 1 John 1:8-10 teach about Jesus' forgiveness?

If we will admit that we sin -
confess - he will forgive
punish us.

Just as Jesus forgave sin when He walked upon the earth, He still forgives all who will put their trust in Him. No matter how terrible your sin may be, you have the promise of 1 John 1:9: If you confess your sin, He will forgive and will cleanse you. Christians do not have to be weighed down with guilt. We can claim the forgiveness of Jesus and realize that through accepting Him, we are holy and blameless in God's sight (see Ephesians 1:4,7).

Take a few minutes to examine your heart. If you have any unconfessed sin standing between you and God, confess it right now. Then claim the forgiveness that is yours in Christ Jesus. Thank God that He sees you as holy and blameless because of Jesus' sacrifice of love. If you have difficulty believing that God can or would forgive you, ask a mature Christian to pray with you.

EXTENDING FORGIVENESS TO OTHERS

According to Colossians 3:12-14, what character qualities do God's people need to exhibit?

Compassion, Kindness, humility, gentleness + patience, love,

What instructions are given regarding forgiveness?

Forgive as the Lord forgave you.

What does it mean to "forgive as the Lord forgave you" (verse 13)?

God accepts us as we are — He recognizes our sin but forgives us our transgressions against Him.

What quality needs to be added to bring perfect unity?

LOVE

What does Matthew 6:14-15 teach about forgiving others and receiving forgiveness from God?

When they sin against you forgive them otherwise you will not be forgiven by the Father

It is important to realize that a bitter, unforgiving spirit shows a serious break in our relationship with God. Those who will not forgive others cannot experience the forgiveness of God. As a result, the unforgiving person will often have tremendous feelings of guilt. As long as we refuse to forgive, we continue to experience the hurts, leaving the door open for Satan to outwit us (see 2 Corinthians 2:5-11). An unforgiving heart is dangerous, not only damaging the person who is unforgiven, but also the one who refuses to forgive. When we choose forgiveness, we free God to begin His work of healing in our lives.

Take a few moments to ask God to show you any lack of forgiveness that is hindering your relationship with Him or with others. Record in your journal what God shows you. Write a prayer asking Him to help you want to forgive that other person. Remember that He wants you to forgive, and He will empower you to do it.

How Unresolved Anger Hinders Forgiveness

It is clear that Scripture commands us to forgive, and those who have forgiven clearly testify of the freedom and healing that forgiveness brings. One of the primary hindrances to forgiveness and to feelings of love is unresolved anger. In fact, unresolved anger in one relationship will often hinder your ability to love in another relationship. For example, unresolved anger toward a parent often hinders one's ability to love a spouse. Let's look at what Scripture teaches about the dangers of anger.

In Ephesians 4:25-32, what instructions does Paul give regarding anger?

do not sin in your anger, do not
let the sun go down while still
angry - don't give Satan a foothold
get rid of anger

What does the phrase "in your anger, do not sin" (verse 26) imply about anger?

that anger is not an emotion from God.
anger can lead to sin if expressed
for wrong reasons

Anger is a natural human emotion that in itself is not sin. Even Jesus, the perfect Son of God, expressed anger (see Mark 3:5; 10:14), and the Old Testament often speaks of God's anger against sin and injustice. Anger is an intense emotion during which our physical body produces extra adrenaline. This adrenaline surge makes anger a very powerful emotion that can be used in healthy and constructive ways, but more often results in sinful and destructive behavior. Because anger is such an intense emotion, we need to be aware of its dangerous potential. What we do with our anger determines whether or not it becomes sin.

What sinful tendency in handling anger does Ephesians 4:26 warn against?

STAYing angry — to not let Something go.

What is the result of the improper handling of anger (see verse 27)?

you give the devil a foothold

How can holding on to anger give Satan a foothold in your life?

you get stuck in a cycle of sin. bitterness invades your being. Its hard to love when you are bitter

What guidelines regarding your speech are given in verse 29?

do not speak unwholesome words. Speak only what is helpful in building up others + will benefit People

How can those guidelines help you resolve anger?

Put others before yourself. Look @ God + His example.

Because anger is such an intense emotion, there is great potential to speak hurtful or abusive language. As Paul dealt with this critical issue, he warned against unwholesome talk that tears people down, rather than building them up. What we say and how we say it will often play a key role in determining whether a relationship is restored or damaged further. Words that are beneficial to others will help restore relationships.

What are we urged to avoid in Ephesians 4:30?

Do not grieve the Holy Spirit

How can inappropriate handling of anger grieve the Holy Spirit?

Goes against the very nature of God

What sinful tendencies in handling anger are we urged to eliminate (see verse 31)?

bitterness, rage, anger, brawling, slander + every form of malice

This passage clearly points out some of the ways in which anger can and does become sinful. If you hang on to anger and do not resolve it quickly, it easily turns into bitterness and will greatly hinder your ability to love. In much the same way, if your anger leads to abusive talk, rage, brawling, slander or malice, the anger has clearly become sinful and destructive to your relationships. Anger can be a hindrance to love, and we must all learn to deal with it in healthy ways.

According to Psalm 39:1-3, what good intentions did David have in keeping silent?

he didn't want to say anything harmful or hurtful

What was the unfortunate result of suppressing his anger?

he meditated on - replaying what happened - anger built until he spoke out

Knowing the dangerous potential of expressing anger, many Christians (like David) try to refrain from expressing their negative emotions altogether. Unfortunately, burying anger usually results in increased anguish, just as David experienced. Unspoken and unresolved anger eats away at the soul, distorting perspective and destroying our ability to love. Communication is often a key to working through the conflict, resolving the anger and coming into a healthy relationship.

According to Ephesians 4:15, what important principle do we need to apply to relationships?

Speak the truth in love

What will be the result?

We will grow in Christ

When expressing anger, you need to carefully apply the principle of "speaking the truth in love" (verse 15). Words spoken in anger have tremendous potential to destroy because they often attack the one who is the object of the anger. You must learn to express your hurts and emotions without attacking. You must also be sensitive to the hurts the other person may be experiencing. It is vital that you talk and listen to each other.

When attempting to resolve anger, you first need to pray; then in an attitude of humility and kindness you need to go to the other person involved. Realize that you may have also inflicted pain on that person. Therefore, you must take responsibility for your role in the conflict and ask forgiveness for any pain you might have caused. If you only confront by voicing your hurts and disappointments, you might get rid of your anger, but in the process you leave the other individual feeling bitter and angry. God's plan is that we be united by a love that forgives, rather than being divided by anger.

A Closer Look at My Own Heart

How important is it that you forgive? Most people want to love, and they desire healthy relationships. Regrettably, many who desire loving relationships still hold on to areas of unforgiveness because they fear that forgiveness will open the door for additional pain.

To forgive does not mean you cannot take a stand against future sin nor set some healthy boundaries. Remember that *agape* love always seeks the highest good for the other individual, and setting healthy boundaries may be in the best interest of everyone involved. Likewise, forgiveness does not mean pretending you were not hurt. Often you must acknowledge the hurt and take it to God before you can really forgive from the heart.

As you study the following passages, ask God to show you the importance of forgiveness in your relationships. Take a few moments and ask God to show you any unresolved anger or lack of forgiveness with which you need to deal.

What question did Peter ask in Matthew 18:21-22?

how many times shall I forgive my
brother who sins against me?
_up to 7?_

What does the question show about Peter?

He isn't allowing God
to be in control

How many times did Jesus say we should forgive?

_77_

Peter may have asked the question regarding how many times he needed to forgive to justify not having to forgive in the future. Perhaps he had already forgiven seven times and felt that was sufficient. Although translators differ as to whether Jesus told Peter to forgive 77 times (*NIV*) or 70 times 7 (*KJV, NEB, RSV*), Jesus was most likely implying that Peter needed to quit counting and keep on forgiving. Perhaps God is also asking you to do the same.

Read Matthew 18:23-27. How much did the first servant owe the king?

10 thousand bags of gold

What did the king order to repay the debt (see verse 25)?

that the man, wife + children be sold to pay the debt

How did the servant react to this order (see verse 26)?

he fell on his knees + begged for mercy

How did the king respond to the servant's plea (see verse 27)?

he took pity on him + cancelled the debt + let him go

It is important to note that 10,000 talents represented an enormous amount of money, equal to millions of dollars in today's economy. There was no way that this servant could have repaid such a huge debt. It was only the goodness of a merciful master that totally cancelled the debt and set him free.

Read Matthew 18:28-35. How much did the fellow servant owe the first servant?

a hundred silver coins

In contrast to the huge debt the first servant owed, the 100 denarii represented only a few dollars. How did he treat the man who owed him the relatively small sum of money?

he choked him + demanded payment He would not release him from the debt

What effect did his lack of forgiveness have on the man who owed him?

he went to prison

How did the fellow servants respond to what they saw?

Outrage

How was the master affected?

The master called the servant to him - He was angry

How did this man's lack of forgiveness destroy him?

By not showing mercy, he recieved none

Just as the lack of his own willingness to forgive left this ungrateful man tortured and imprisoned, people who refuse to forgive find themselves in tormented bondage. The consequences of not forgiving are widespread and severe. This man's lack of forgiveness impacted the one owing him money, his fellow servants and the king. However, the one most severely affected was the man himself. The master had given him freedom, but because of his own unforgiving attitude, that freedom was taken away and he was placed in prison.

Because God in His mercy has forgiven us, He expects us to be merciful and forgiving toward others. Refusal to forgive leaves us locked in the pain and unable to experience freedom in Christ. The most unhappy people on earth are those who will not forgive. Hanging on to our grievances always carries severe consequences.

What consequence of not forgiving is found in Matthew 18:35?
He went to jail - He was seperated

This verse points out the terrible spiritual consequences of refusing to forgive. Those who refuse to forgive are unable to relate to God because of the bitterness in their hearts, and often that bitterness is passed on to children and grandchildren. In addition, there are physical and emotional consequences because the lack of forgiveness creates a greater susceptibility toward illnesses and depression. Regrettably, there are also social consequences; bitterness toward one person will hinder your relationship with another, and you will tend to become like the one you resent. Failing to forgive prevents the emotional and spiritual healing of the hurts and surrenders the power to attain happiness in your life to the offender.

The good news is that you can *choose* to forgive. With God's help, you can gain the power you need to forgive from the depths of your innermost being. You do not have to *feel* like forgiving before you forgive. If you wait for feelings, you will never forgive! You forgive because God requires it and because it is in your own best interest.

Action Steps I Can Take Today

Determine that you will quickly resolve anger in healthy ways. The following steps can be used any time you are having difficulty resolving anger:

- Give yourself permission to express anger in healthy ways.

- Identify the root emotion. Anger is a secondary emotion. Often what you are feeling is actually hurt, fear, embarrassment or another emotion.

- Give yourself time for the intensity of the anger to dissipate before addressing the situation. If you react too quickly, you may say or do things in the heat of the moment that will damage the relationship and lead to regret.

- Do something physical to dissipate the adrenaline, such as taking a brisk walk or jog, working in the yard, and so on. This will help you to be in better control when you ultimately express the anger.

- Ask for God's help in resolving the situation. Praying aloud may be especially helpful in working through the intensity of the emotion before addressing the situation.

- Express the anger in healthy ways. This means calmly expressing the anger at the action without attacking the person. Express the primary emotion you felt (i.e., fear, hurt, and so on) and avoid use of the words "always" and "never."

- Forgive the offender.

Take the following steps toward forgiveness:

- *Choose to forgive.* Remember that forgiveness is a decision you make to obey God. If you will set your will to forgive, God will give you the emotional strength to be able to forgive from your heart.

- *Ask God to show you what He wants you to learn from this situation.* God has allowed this situation for some purpose, and He will bring good from every difficulty in your life if you will let Him. Record in your journal anything God reveals to you.

- *Ask God to give you His power to forgive.* Sometimes you may need to ask God for the desire to forgive; but remember that forgiveness is His will for you and that He will give you the grace and the power to do it when you sincerely ask for His help. Write a prayer requesting this power in your journal.

- *Pray for the offender.* Ask God to show you how you can best pray for this person and record in your journal what He shows you. Pray for the individual any time feelings of anger or hurt resurface.

- *Ask God to show you if you need to express forgiveness to the other individual.* Sometimes this is helpful, and at other times it may cause the other person more pain. Seek godly counsel from a mature Christian if you are unsure of God's direction.

- *Thank God* for the freedom and the forgiveness that is yours through Jesus Christ our Lord.

FIVE

LOVE IS SACRIFICING AND SERVING

As the pastor paid tribute to his deceased mother, he said, "It was not until I was an adult that I realized her favorite piece of chicken was not the neck." He was raised in a large family during the Great Depression, and meat was not plentiful on the table. When the chicken was passed around, his mother always took the neck. She took it so graciously that he did not realize that she was putting the needs of her family above her own. He thought the almost meatless neck was simply her favorite piece. In many ways his mother had loved with a sacrificial and serving love that cheerfully placed the needs of others above her own.

A Closer Look at the Problem

We live in a society that has been trained to look out for self, trained to make meeting *our own* wants and *our own* needs the number-one priority in life. In our desire for positions of prominence and power, we hope the recognition of our importance will bring the feelings of significance we long for. Serving where there seems to be little recognition or thanks is difficult and seemingly unrewarding.

In sharp contrast to a self-centered society is the sacrificial and serving love of Jesus toward us. He left the splendors of heaven to face rejection, to suffer and ultimately die in order to meet our greatest need. His kind of love is never self-centered or arrogant. If we are to love as Jesus loves us, we must also learn to love with a love that is willing to serve and give sacrificially. Here is the threefold focus for this lesson:

1. To recognize and appreciate the sacrificial love of Jesus toward you.
2. To see how Jesus gave you an example of serving love in action.

3. To learn how you can overcome the natural human tendency toward selfishness and reach out to others with a serving and sacrificial love.

As you begin your study, ask God to open your heart to more fully grasp His love, which will empower you to love others. Ask Him to help you recognize any areas of selfishness that are hindering the growth of love in your life.

A Closer Look at God's Truth

Jesus' Sacrificing Love

In John 15:9-15, what does Jesus promise those who keep His commands?

that we will remain in Jesus' love

What did Jesus command us to do (see verse 12)?

Love each other as Jesus has loved us

What does Jesus describe as the greatest expression of love?

to lay down your life to another

How is Jesus' entire life a demonstration of that kind of love?

He came to earth knowing what He would have to do. He chose to go to the cross for us.

Read 1 John 4:9-12. How did God show His love for us (see verse 9)?

He sent His one + only Son into this world

How does verse 10 define love?

love is God loving us + Sent Jesus as an atoning sacrifice for our sins

What should be the result of receiving God's great love for us (see verse 11)?

We ought to love one another

What shows when we love each other (see verse 12)?

God

How does accepting God's love make it easier to love one another?

We know we are not pefect + Sin + if God Can love me - I Can love others.

Jesus gave up the glory and the adoration that was His in heaven to become one of us. His love brought Him to earth that we might enjoy abundant and eternal life. He was rejected, beaten, spit upon, mocked and crucified to enable us to come into a right relationship with God. His willingness to bear excruciating physical pain and carry the unspeakable shame of mankind's sin and guilt demonstrates His incredible love for us. When we accept Jesus as Savior and Lord, His love becomes active within us. As we allow His Spirit to control us, His love at work in us willingly reaches out to others with sacrificial love.

Read Ephesians 5:1-2. What instructions are given in verse 1?

Follow Gods example

What does it mean to imitate God as His "dearly loved children"?

_____
_____
_____
_____

What kind of life are we to live?

_____the way of love_____
_____
_____
_____

How are we instructed to love?

_____As chnst loved us_____
_____
_____

How does loving with a sacrificial love relate to being an imitator of God?

_____God first Sacnficed for us._____
_____
_____

Children are fantastic imitators, loving to play dress-up and pretend they are Mommy or Daddy. Through imitation, they quickly master language skills and often reflect their parents' behavior. In the same way, God wants our lives to imitate His expression of sacrificial love toward us. What are some practical actions of sacrificial love that can be demonstrated in today's culture?

_____Patience, Not having to be nght all
the time, forgiveness, Grace,
understanding_____
_____

How would sacrificial love relate to the use of your time?

_____Ding for others - using my
time for someone else_____
_____
_____

How would it relate to your money?

You should share with others

How would it relate to your home and other possessions?

Your possessions shouldn't be more important than people

How would it relate to your energy?

The term "sacrificial" implies that there is a significant cost involved in what one is giving. This usually means giving beyond what is comfortable and easy. People who are hungry for love and attention may need more of our time or energy than we can comfortably give. Sacrificial love may require that we open our homes, share our finances or in some other way become involved in meeting their needs. Sacrificial love must be accomplished in and through the power of Jesus. Attempting to love sacrificially in one's own strength too often results in fatigue, resentment and burnout.

THE SERVING LOVE OF JESUS

In John 13:1-5, what did Jesus know, according to verse 1?

that the hour had come for Him to leave the world & go to his father

What did He show His disciples?

Love

What was Jesus' position and authority?

the Father had put all things under his power

What action of love did Jesus perform?

He washed the disciples feet

What did Jesus' washing of the disciples' feet show?

humility, Love — he acted as their servant

How did His willingness to become a servant relate to His greatness?

he came to serve us + serve us without resentment

As Jesus ate with His disciples on the night before He was to be crucified, there was much they needed to learn about true greatness. As humans, they were prone to the common practice of comparing themselves with each other, and they wanted to hold the most important positions in the Savior's kingdom.

The task of washing feet was traditionally done by the lowliest of the household servants, and none of the disciples appeared willing to do such a menial task. Yet, Jesus, the Lord and Master, showed His great love to His disciples by taking the position of the lowliest servant and performing the humblest of acts.

Luke 22:24-27 records a discussion that took place that very same night. What was the subject of the dispute?

Which of the disciples would be the greatest

According to these verses, how do the Gentiles (or unbelievers) view greatness?

that greatness makes you better than others

How are Christians to be different in their views of greatness?

be willing to serve, be willing to be last

What do you think Jesus meant when He said, "The greatest among you should be like the youngest, and the one who rules like the one who serves" (verse 26)?

We should be willing to be last and to serve others without resentment

How did Jesus describe Himself (see verse 27)?

servant - one who serves

Perhaps the disciples' discussion prompted Jesus' practical demonstration of servant love. He contrasted the world's view of greatness, in which power and prominence appear to equal greatness, with God's view, in which serving others denotes greatness. In a culture that honored the elderly, the youngest would have been the one who traditionally served the others and would have been considered the least significant. By contrast, Jesus indicated that the greatest in His kingdom would be the one who willingly serves others.

Read John 13:12-17. What had the disciples called Jesus?

TEACHER AND Lord

What was His response to those titles (see verse 13)?

he acknowledged that both of those titles are correct

What instructions did Jesus give (see verses 14-15)?

Wash others feet - follow Jesus example

What truth was Jesus emphasizing in verse 16?

that we are all equal but God is above all

What promise is given for those who obey these instructions?

They will be blessed

How does this passage apply to Christians today?

We must recognize Jesus + God's authority. Follow Jesus' example + serve others

What are some practical ways that we can serve each other?

helpout with physical needs - provide food, Clothing. Take care of others, teach

How do you feel when you do something to help someone?

It makes me feel good

In washing the disciples' feet, Jesus gave all believers a beautiful example of love in action. Love willingly becomes a servant. Love does not seek to exalt self, but to serve others. Rather than asking, *How much must I do?* serving love asks, *What more can I do?*

We often try to exalt ourselves just as the disciples did. Verse 17 emphasizes that it is as we serve others that we are blessed. When we serve others, our own sense of self-worth grows. It is in humbling ourselves and serving others that we are exalted.

Read Matthew 25:31-40. List the phrases commending those who were to inherit the kingdom.

vs 35 - 36

Why did the words of the King surprise those who had served others (see verses 37-39)?

B/C they were serving people or so they thought people

How did Jesus view those actions done for others?

What you do for a brother/sister of Christ you are doing for Him

How might verse 40 be a motivation for us to serve others?

We can see it as serving God — not lowering ourselves to serve an equal someone we see as

From Matthew 25:41-46, list phrases telling what these individuals had failed to do.

did not feed, or give something to drink did not invite in, did not clothe him, did not visit in prison

How did Jesus view their lack of action?

that they didn't love them

It is interesting that neither group in this parable thought of their service or lack of service as unto Jesus, but that is the way He described both. The first group was not saved through their actions, but their loving service to others demonstrated God's Spirit at work within them. The lack of loving actions in the second group showed they did not really even know God. They thought they did, but their lack of genuine concern proved otherwise.

How does Galatians 5:13 instruct us regarding our use of freedom and its relationship to love?

use your freedom to humbly serve one another in love

Through Jesus' loving sacrifice, we have been set free from the power of sin and the burden of legalism. However, that freedom should never be used as an excuse for sinful behavior. Instead, we are called to serve each other in love. In Galatians 5:13, the Greek word translated "love" is once again *agape*, which denotes a giving, serving love that always seeks the highest good for the other individual.

A Closer Look at My Own Heart

For most of us, sacrificial giving or joyfully serving others does not come naturally. Yet there is tremendous power in this kind of love. As you study the remaining passages, ask God to show you how applying the principles given in these verses would affect your relationships. Ask Him to show you changes in attitudes and actions that would help you to grow in Christlike love.

If you are struggling to love a specific person, ask God to show you ways that you can serve that person. As you willingly seek to serve and to meet that person's needs, your feelings are given an atmosphere of love in which to grow.

As you read Philippians 2:1-11, list the actions and attitudes that are encouraged. (Note: the Greek word translated "if" in verse 1 can also be translated "since.")

Comfort, unity, tenderness + compassion,
value "others" above yourself, love

Which of these actions and attitudes are strengths for you?

_?_

What attitudes and actions are discouraged?

? Selfish Ambition, vain Conceit
not looking to your own interests

Which are weaknesses that point to areas of needed growth?

How is Jesus described in verse 6?

did not Consider equality with
God to be used to his
own advantage

Which phrases show what Jesus became for us?

_VS 7-8_

Which phrases show that Jesus had a choice?

Obedient -
he made himself nothing

What qualities did Paul encourage when he urged the Philippians (and us) to have the same attitude Jesus had?

be like Minded, Love,
one in Spirit + be one mind

How does this passage relate to the renewing of the mind (see Romans 12:1-2)?

We are called not to
Conform to the pattern
of this world

What are some practical actions you can take to renew your mind and develop Christlike attitudes?

pray, read the bible, reject
negative thinking, spend time
with believers who are like
Minded

How would your relationships be changed if you were to use Philippians 2:3-8 as your guide?

more intimate - happier - not as
much discord

What changes do you need to make to put these verses into practice?

Renew my mind, practice
praying for others
be consistent

How did God reward the sacrificial and serving actions of Jesus?
RAISED him from the Dead

Jesus' actions are the ultimate example of sacrificial and serving love. Sometimes it is difficult to serve others or serve in lowly positions, because we feel it lessens our significance as individuals. The struggle for feelings of significance and importance may hinder our willingness to serve others. By contrast, Jesus knew full well who and what He was. Lacking any struggle regarding His own identity and significance, He was able to freely serve others.

It will be difficult to respond with Jesus' kind of love unless you first recognize who and what you are in Jesus. You are God's deeply loved child, so valuable to Him that He sent His Son to bring you into a right relationship with Himself. As you more fully grasp how precious you are to God, He assures you of your personal significance and importance. Then He works in you to develop the same attitudes that Jesus had. This involves spending time with Him, feeding on His Word and allowing His Holy Spirit the freedom to change your way of thinking. You must honestly look at your self-seeking and self-serving attitudes and ask God to change your heart.[1]

Often when struggling in a relationship, part of the problem is that we allow our minds to dwell on our own unmet needs. Focusing on our unfulfilled needs tends to magnify their importance and we become increasingly dissatisfied in our relationships. Changing our focus from our unmet needs to honestly seeking to do what will be best for others and meeting their true needs is necessary for a healthy relationship.

When you seek to meet the needs of others, you will often find your own needs are also being met or God will graciously change your needs to bring you peace and satisfaction in any situation. By contrast, if you make meeting your needs your number-one priority, those needs will rarely be met and you will continue to feel unsatisfied. When you seek to meet the needs of others, you usually find joy, contentment and feelings of love growing within you.

Action Steps I Can Take Today

Spend time praising God that He sees you as significant and extremely valuable. Remember, it was His great love for the whole world that led to the sacrificial death of Jesus. To help you more fully accept your personal significance, read the following passages and record in your journal what each says about your position in Christ:

- John 1:12 *Believer become Children of God*
- Romans 8:1-2 *no comdemnation for those in Christ Jesus*
- Romans 8:35-39 *nothing will seperate us from the love of God*
- 1 Corinthians 6:19-20 *our bodies are temples of the Holy Spirit*
- Ephesians 2:4-6 *Gods grace has saved us.*
- Ephesians 2:18-19 *We are fellow citizens with Gods People + are members of his household*

Thank Him that the truth indicated in each of these passages is true for you.

Ask God to show you any actions or attitudes that demonstrate selfishness in your relationships. Record in your journal what He reveals to you.

In your journal, write a prayer giving God permission to change you. Ask Him to renew your mind and help you grow in Christlike attitudes and actions.

Recognize that actions that convey love to you may not necessarily convey love to another individual. If you are seeking to strengthen a love relationship, consider asking the other person, "What communicates love to you?" Then determine to act upon what you learn.

Ask God to show you specific actions of serving love that He wants you to perform. Make a list of the actions He shows you; then record the date you perform each serving act.

Note

1. For additional study on renewing your mind, see *Transformed by God's Word* in the Women of the Word Bible Study series (Ventura, CA: Gospel Light, 2010).

SIX

ℒOVE IS KIND AND UPLIFTING

Emotionally beaten down and never affirmed in his early childhood, Brian had responded by withdrawing into himself and believing that he was very stupid. Later he was sent to live with grandparents who lovingly accepted him. They showered him with kindness, and their words affirmed his value. Gradually, the wounds began to heal, and he wrote a letter declaring, "I'm not stupid anymore." The power of lovingkindness had touched his life and built him up.

A Closer Look at the Problem

Life is sometimes cruel and painful. Disappointments can overwhelm, leaving us feeling inadequate and insignificant. At such difficult times, kind words and deeds can sustain and bring hope. Everyone wants to be treated with kindness; without it life becomes painful and burdensome.

In this chapter, we will see that Jesus' love demonstrates kindness. If we are to love as Jesus loves us, treating others kindly is essential. Sometimes this is easy and other times it may be extremely difficult. One of the most needed acts of kindness is that of building each other up. The sinful nature is quick to attack and tear others down, leaving individuals struggling with low self-esteem. We all need someone who will reach out to us with kindness and an uplifting attitude. Here is the dual focus of this lesson:

1. To recognize and accept the lovingkindness of the Lord toward you.
2. To choose words and actions of kindness that will reach out to others with love that builds them up.

Before you begin, ask God to make you aware of any unkindness toward others in your life. Will you ask Him to teach you how to replace unkind words and deeds with actions that are kind and uplifting?

A Closer Look at God's Truth

GOD'S KINDNESS TOWARD US

In Jeremiah 31:3-4, how is God's love described?

Everlasting - unfailing

As you read 1 Corinthians 13:4-7, list the actions that describe kindness.

patient, kind, does not envy, does not boast, not proud, not self-seeking, does not dishonor others, not easily angered, no record of wrongs, rejoices in the truth protects, trusts, hopes perseveres

How did Jesus' love demonstrate kindness in the following passages?

Matthew 19:13-15

He said the kingdom of Heaven belonged to children, placed his hands on them + prayed

Mark 5:25-34

He healed a woman + spoke kindly to her

Luke 5:12-13

he willingly healed a man who had leprosy

What do the following verses reveal about God's love and His kindness?

Psalm 63:3

His love is better than life

Ephesians 2:4-7

His love is rich in mercy

Titus 3:4-7

His love is merciful, generous

List some ways that you have personally benefited from God's lovingkindness toward you.

As you more fully grasp the nature of God's love for you, you will find greater freedom to risk loving others with kindness that will build them up. If you have difficulty believing that God is kind or that He directs His kindness toward you, ask a more mature Christian to pray with you about that issue.

GOD'S KINDNESS TOUCHES OTHERS THROUGH HIS CHILDREN
According to 2 Peter 1:3-4, what has God in His kindness given to us?

— everything we need for a godly life
— his great + precious promises

What key to power is described in verse 3?

through our knowledge of him.

How do verses 3 and 4 promise the strength to live a life of love?

We can escape the corruption in the world.
He has given us everything we need to live a godly life

What role does God's Spirit play in living that life of victory?

We have to allow His spirit to be in charge

What do you think the phrase "through our knowledge of him" means (verse 3)?

Spend time with him in prayer, read the BIBLE

How can we grow in our knowledge of Him?

READ THE BIBLE
CLASSES
PRAYER

If you personally know Jesus as Savior and Lord, God promises everything you need to live a life of godliness. This means His divine power is at work in you and enables you to rise above the world's corruption and live a life of love. To grow in your knowledge of Him, you must spend time with Him, sharing your struggles and listening to His voice. Spending time studying His Word will help you know His heart; and as you obey His voice, you will grow in your knowledge of Him (see John 14:21).

we must keep His commands

In 2 Peter 1:5-9, which phrase indicates the individual's responsibility in Christian growth?

we must add to our faith: goodness, knowledge, self control, perseverance, godliness, mutual affection, love. We must continue to grow

What character qualities need to be added to faith?

See above

Which phrase in verse 8 implies a growing Christian?

increasing measure

What is the result of these qualities growing in your life?

Keep us from being ineffective + unproductive in your knowledge of Jesus.

What steps can you take to add these qualities to your life and help them to grow?

Seek to see what God says about each quality, ask God to help you grow. Read

How does unkindness keep a Christian from being effective and productive?

Yes. Then we can't see past ourselves + in doing so keeps others from seeing Jesus

How can kindness increase your effectiveness?

People will see your love for them + be able to see God in you

Even though God has given you everything you need to live a godly life, part of the responsibility for your growth rests upon you. Growth is not automatic, and you must do your part to grow in godly attributes. If you will draw into His presence and submit yourself to Him, you will increase in your knowledge of Him and will grow in godliness. Your ability to treat others with lovingkindness will increase as you more fully grasp His great love for you.

What qualities does 2 Timothy 2:22-24 say you should pursue?

righteousness, faith, love, peace

Describe some ways an individual could pursue these qualities.

Seek out other believers -
ask God to help you
grow, read the Bible

Why is it important to pursue these qualities "along with those who call on the Lord out of a pure heart" (verse 22)?

to be used for Gods greater
glory

What kinds of arguments are you to avoid, and why?

foolish + stupid - no value
in the argument

Do you feel that all arguments are foolish and stupid? Why or why not?

No, sometimes you are arguing
for the greater Good, Gods
good

What is the difference between an argument and a quarrel?

argument - exchange of views usually angry
quarrel a angry argument

How can quarreling lead to unkindness and resentfulness?

If you can't agree to disagree you may disrespect the other person which may lead to more unkind words or behavior

How can quarreling make one's teaching ineffective?

If you can't listen + then speak in love people may stop listening to you

When the apostle Paul wrote to young Timothy, he shared principles that would help him succeed as an effective pastor and teacher. In urging Timothy to pursue righteousness, faith, love and peace, Paul implies that these important qualities are somewhat elusive, and achieving them will require effort.

Foolish arguments will quickly undermine the growth of these godly qualities. Arguments in and of themselves are not necessarily foolish. For example, the apostle Paul often presented arguments proving that Jesus was the Messiah (see Acts 9:22; 17:2-4; 18:4). However, there are many unnecessary arguments over inconsequential matters that lead to quarreling. The Greek word translated as "quarrels" in these verses implies anger and strife. These types of arguments need to be avoided because they are destructive to the kingdom of God.

What qualities does 2 Timothy 2:24 say the Lord's servant should possess?

Kind to everyone, able to teach, not resentful

In your life, who are the people you are teaching?

Sometimes your kids, people who don't know God

Why is kindness so important if you are going to be an effective teacher?

People want to be respected
If you want people to listen
to you its best to be kind

Paul also urged kindness in all of God's servants. Kindness is an essential factor in our effectiveness as teachers, whether in our churches, jobs or homes. We need to realize that every Christian has a realm of influence, and we are teaching through our attitudes, words and actions.

Unfortunately, too often our attitudes and actions are contrary to what we are trying to teach with our words. When this is true, our teachings become hollow and ineffective. For example, a child will be far more receptive to learning spiritual truths from a kind parent than from one who is unkind. The effectiveness of anyone who is trying to teach about God will be limited unless that individual's teaching is combined with actions of kindness. Regrettably, a lack of kindness in the teacher often leads to rejection of the teaching altogether.

In Titus 2:3-5, what was Titus encouraged to teach the older women?

to be reverent in the way they live

What were the older women to teach the younger women?

love their husbands + children,
to be self-controlled + pure,
to be busy @ home, to be kind
to be subject to their
husbands

What would be the result of the women learning these things?

Kingdom of God growing

What do you think is meant by the phrase "so that no one will malign the word of God" (verse 5)?

If we don't live out the word of God people will assume what the Bible says isn't true

How do unkind actions bring disrespect to God?

It causes unbelief

How does kindness bring God glory?

It reflects God.

THE POWER OF WORDS
Kindness is described in Scripture as both an action of love and a fruit of the Spirit (see 1 Corinthians 13:4 and Galatians 5:22). One important way you can express kindness is through loving words. As you study the following passages, let God speak to you regarding the impact of your words.

According to 1 Corinthians 8:1, what does love do?

Love builds up.

How does that action relate to your words?

Words can either be kind + loving or not. You can build someone up verbally

In 1 Thessalonians 5:8-11, what qualities are you encouraged to have?
Sober, Faith, love, hope
receive salvation, encourager

What words imply these qualities are a protection?
Protect us from wrath

How can you increase in those qualities?

What actions should be a result of God's love toward you (see verse 11)?
Encourage one another +
build one another up.

What are some practical ways to apply the instructions in verse 11?
speak truth in love, give compliments,
do not slander

How does verse 11 relate to your words?
Kind words

What do the following verses teach you about the power of your words?

Proverbs 12:18
reckless words can hurt
but wise | kind words can heal

Proverbs 15:1
speaking gently can avoid
a fight whereas harsh
unkind words can stir up
anger

Proverbs 15:4
soothing tongue - tree of life
perverse tongue - crushes the
spirit

Proverbs 16:24
Gracious words are sweet
to the soul & healing to
the bones

Proverbs 18:21
tongue has power of
life + death

2 Timothy 2:16
Avoid godless chatter

Words can be loving and kind, or they can be brutal and destructive. Words can build up, or they can tear down. Often the people who are the most difficult to love are those with low self-esteem. They are incapable of reaching out in love to others because they do not love themselves. One of the most needed actions of love toward those people is the need to build them up.

If you know such a person, ask God to show you his or her actions for which you can honestly be grateful. Tell that individual how much you appreciate each of the good qualities that God shows you. Expressing appreciation in this way will help you to focus upon the best in that person and it will encourage and build him or her up.

A Closer Look at My Own Heart

Take a few moments to honestly evaluate your speech. Ask yourself the following questions:

- Does my speech usually bring healing or does it often wound?
- Does it bring life or does it crush the spirit?
- Do my words turn away wrath or do they stir up anger?
- Is my speech godless chatter that leads to greater ungodliness, or just the opposite?
- Are my words pleasant or harsh?

Ask God to show you areas of needed improvement as you answer the following questions.

According to Ephesians 4:29-32, what kind of talk should not come out of your mouth? *Unwholesome talk*

What should your words accomplish (see verse 29)? *helpful in building up others — so it will benifit them*

What actions of love are described in verse 32? *Be kind + compassionate forgive one another*

When do your words grieve the Holy Spirit?

Un wholesome talk

get rid of all bitterness, rage - anger
malice

How do verses 31 and 32 relate to your words?

Our words can build up or tear
down

Write a paraphrase of verses 29 through 32, personalizing these instructions to make them applicable to your life and your words.

Do not speak unkindly about anyone -
Whether to their face or not.
Think before you speak. Seek out God.
Ask for forgiveness.

As you make the building up of another person your goal, that person often begins to feel better about himself or herself and often becomes easier to love. When you seek to build up another person, God will also give you increased feelings of love toward that person. Will you choose today to reach out to others with a love that is kind and builds up?

Action Steps I Can Take Today

Take time to consider God's lovingkindness toward you. In your journal, make a list of the different ways that God has shown kindness to you and your loved ones. Then write a prayer of praise, thanking God for His lovingkindness.

Evaluate your recent conversations. Think back over your discussions of the past week. In your journal, list the times when your conversation has been helpful to others and the times when it has been harmful.

Ask God to reveal to you any areas of unwholesome talk in your life and record in your journal the areas God reveals to you. Write a prayer confessing that unwholesome talk as sin and ask God to give you His strength to overcome.

Ask God to give you a specific plan to make your speech more beneficial and useful in building others up. Consider how you can apply the following practical suggestions to help you overcome unwholesome talk:

- Ask for God's help daily. Remember that no man can tame the tongue, but God's Holy Spirit can!
- Don't speak too quickly. Carefully weigh what you will say.
- Speak in ways you want others to speak to you.
- Pretend the recipient is a respected friend or your pastor.
- Think about how you would feel if your conversation were being recorded.
- Refuse to participate in destructive conversation, even as a listener.
- Ask yourself, *What would Jesus say?*
- Carefully guard what goes into your mind, because "out of the abundance of the heart the mouth speaks" (Matthew 12:34, *NKJV*).

Record in your journal what you plan to do to make your speech more beneficial.

Ask God to show you someone who needs your encouragement today and reveal practical ways that you can build that person up. Write in your journal any thoughts God reveals to you; then choose to follow His leading. As you respond to God's leading, record the dates along with the actions you are taking.

Ask God to show you practical acts of kindness that you can do to help build up and encourage the following people:

- Your family members
- Your friends
- Your co-workers
- Others in your church or fellowship

Memorize Psalm 19:14 and make it your daily prayer:

May the words of my mouth and the meditation of my heart
be pleasing in your sight,
O LORD, my Rock and my Redeemer.

SEVEN

ℒOVE IS DISCERNING

Jim and Louise loved their wayward daughter, Karen, and grieved as they watched her descend into the pit of drug and alcohol addiction. Repeatedly, they tried to help by paying bills, caring for her children and covering for her irresponsible behavior. Unfortunately, their efforts did not help Karen out of her addiction, but instead enabled her to stay there. While their love may have been giving, serving and sacrificing, it was lacking in discernment. Eventually, they realized how their actions were contributing to the problem. Jim and Louise arranged an intervention, after which Karen voluntarily entered a treatment center and gained victory over the addiction. Karen needed love that was discerning.

A Closer Look at the Problem

Sometimes love needs to be tough and confrontational. It's easy to identify certain actions such as serving, sacrificing and accepting as actions of love. However, we see that God's love will also confront sin because it is in the best interest of the individual. Discerning love sometimes must say no and set healthy boundaries. *Agape* love that always seeks the highest good for the other individual is a discerning love that will recognize when a person needs tenderness or firmness. Here is the dual focus of this chapter:

1. To discover how God's love toward you is a discerning love.
2. To help you grow in discernment so that your love will result in the highest good for the other individual.

Before you begin your study, will you ask God to show you areas where your love needs to grow in discernment? Will you ask Him to help you apply the truths from these Scriptures to your relationships?

A Closer Look at God's Truth

In Mark 10:17-22, what did this young man's question reveal about him?

That he didn't know what he needed to do to have eternal life

Why did Jesus direct the man's attention to the commandments?

B/C. When we ~~obey~~ love God - we will obey His commandments

What does verse 20 reveal about the young man?

That he felt he was good enough.

Notice that verse 21 says specifically that Jesus "loved him." How did Jesus' love show discernment?

he could tell from what the young man had said & from his appearance what he needed to do

What did Jesus promise if the young man would put God's kingdom first?

You will have treasure in heaven

What did the young man choose, and what was the result of his choice?

He choose himself & his wealth. He had treasure here on earth but not in heaven

In this passage, a rich young man who was also a ruler (see Luke 18:18) approached Jesus seeking the key to eternal life. Not only was the influential young man wealthy, but he also appears to have lived a clean and wholesome life. His parents were probably proud to have him as a son. He had a genuine desire to be right with God, but regretfully, he did not recognize his own sinfulness. In loving discernment, Jesus truthfully confronted him with the change that was essential before he could be right with God. Riches had become more important to him than his relationship with God. Although Jesus loved the young man, He did not lessen His requirements for discipleship. The young man left full of sorrow, knowing that his riches and influence could not bring the peace and the joy he was seeking.

In Hebrews 12:4-11, what do verses 5 and 6 teach us about God's love?

he loves enough to discipline us.
He will rebuke us in love if we are doing wrong

How should we respond to God's discipline?

do not make light of his discipline.
do not lose heart;
Endure - & accept the discipline

What does it show when God does not discipline an individual (see verse 8)?

you are not true sons + daughters at all

How does God's discipline compare to the discipline of a loving parent (see verses 9-10)?

Parents discipline as they think is best - for a little while - God disciplines us so we can share in his holiness.

What are the goals of God's discipline (see verses 9-11)?

to share in Gods holiness - to produce a harvest of righteousness + peace

How does this passage demonstrate the discerning nature of God's love?

He sees our sin + is not afraid to cause pain for our greater good

The Greek verb that is translated as "discipline" in the *New International Version* properly relates to the training of a child and includes instruction, counsel, discipline, correction and chastisement as needed. God will allow us to experience the consequences of wrong actions to draw us back to Him. His love will let us go through difficult and painful circumstances because that is when we are the most likely to grow and mature. His love, which always seeks the good of His children, will bring correction to us when we need it. The following passages tell of a situation in which the apostle Paul had to use a discerning and confronting love.

According to 1 Corinthians 5:1-6, what sin was Paul confronting?

Incest
_____
_____
_____

What had been the attitude of the church (see verses 2,6)?

Proud, boastful, ignoring the sin
_____
_____

What attitudes should they have had?

been disgusted + willing to stand
up for what was happening
_____
_____

What disciplinary action did Paul urge them to take in regard to this man (see verses 2,5)?

put the fellow out of fellowship
hand him over to satan
_____

What was the goal of the discipline that Paul recommended (see verses 5-6)?

destruction of the flesh - spirit
saved
_____
_____
_____

Why do you think Paul urged such drastic treatment of the sinning man?

b/c that was what it was going to take to over come the sin

How does sexual immorality destroy the work of the Lord?

B/c it is sin + not holy, you cannot do the work of God + be sexually immoral they do not go together

Paul wrote to the Corinthians with a heavy heart. Corinth was notorious for its sexual promiscuity and religious prostitution, yet the church in Corinth had allowed blatant immorality of such an extreme nature that even Corinthians who were nonbelievers were shocked. The church had failed to confront the sinning individual and had proudly acted as if nothing were wrong. Paul urged prompt confrontation for the good of the individual and for the sake of the church. Paul expressed concern that this sin could easily spread to the entire fellowship.

Notice that there are actually two instances of confrontation in this passage. While Paul urged the church to deal with this man's sin, he also confronted the church regarding their attitudes and their lack of disciplinary action. The following passages will show the results of these confrontations.

THE POSITIVE EFFECTS OF LOVING CONFRONTATION
In 2 Corinthians 7:2-7, which words express Paul's love for the Corinthians (see verse 3)?

verse He would live or die for them

How does he affirm them (see verse 4)?

That we do not have authority over our own body but must yield to our spouse he is encouraged

How does Paul describe himself in verses 5-6?

_He has had no rest he's
been harrassed - he's downcast
but comforted_

Why do you think Paul was in such turmoil?

_B/c he was preaching things
that were uncomfortable
to hear it they made his
life hard_

What had comforted Paul (see verses 6-7)?

God + the coming of Titus

When Paul arrived in Macedonia, he had no idea how the Corinthian church had reacted to his letter. Not knowing whether they had responded to his plea or had angrily rebelled against his instructions, he experienced great inner turmoil. Then Titus arrived from Corinth, bringing the good news of the powerful and positive impact of Paul's letter, and assuring him of their love. This news brought the apostle great comfort and joy.

According to 2 Corinthians 7:8-11, what was the reaction to Paul's letter?

_They initially were hurt but it
didn't last long_

Why do you think Paul struggled with feelings of regret?

he didn't want to hurt them

What had the Corinthians' sorrow led them to do?

repent + be saved

What is the difference between "worldly sorrow" and "godly sorrow" (see verse 10)?

worldly sorrow-brings death-focused on ourselves, godly sorrow - we repent b/c we are sorry not to be holy

What had the godly sorrow produced (see verses 10-11)?

earnestness, eagerness to clear themselves, indignation, alarm, longing, concern desire to [justice] to be done

When Paul addressed the blatant sin in the church, it was necessary for him to be stern. Many Bible scholars feel that a third letter, harshly written to the Corinthians (but lost to us), may be the letter Paul refers to in this passage. What is obvious from this passage is that his needing to be harsh in confrontation left him with feelings of regret and turmoil.

We must understand that loving confrontation is not easy! It may leave you wondering if you have destroyed the relationship or if the confrontation is accomplishing anything positive. Fears and doubts may plague you even as they did the apostle Paul.

At the same time, we must recognize the awesome potential of Spirit-led and loving confrontation. The Corinthians had responded with godly sorrow that led to repentance and restoration—these must be the goals of discerning love. By contrast, worldly sorrow, which does not involve repentance, leads to guilt and regret and, ultimately, to spiritual death. Too often worldly sorrow is sorrow at being caught rather than being sorry for sin.

According to 2 Corinthians 2:4-11, what emotions did Paul experience as he wrote the harsh letter?

great distress, anguish of the heart

What was his purpose?

to let them know the depths of his love for them

What actions of love does he urge toward the sinning man at this point?

forgive & comfort him
reaffirm your love to him

Why does he urge forgiveness (see verses 7-8,11)?

B/C God calls us to forgive
So he can forgive us.

Do you feel the man had repented of his immorality? Why or why not?

No B/C Paul had to address
the Corinthians again

Although these verses do not specifically say that the man had repented, it is highly unlikely that Paul would have encouraged the church to forgive and to receive him without an obvious change in behavior. It appears the church had taken the bold disciplinary actions that Paul had recommended and this individual had then responded in repentance. Following repentance, discerning love needed to add forgiveness to restore that individual to fellowship where he could grow and mature in his Christian walk. *Repentance and restoration are always the goal of discerning love.*

A CALL TO THE MINISTRY OF RESTORATION

According to Galatians 6:1-3, what should we do when a fellow Christian falls into sin?

What does it mean to "restore that person gently" (verse 1)?

What caution should we take when seeking to restore another believer, and why is this important?

_____

_____

_____

What steps can one take to avoid falling into temptation while helping another individual overcome sin?

_____

_____

_____

_____

What are some practical ways we can apply verse 2 when ministering to a believer who has fallen into sin?

_____

_____

_____

_____

Galatians 6:2 states that carrying another's burdens will "fulfill the law of Christ." To what does the "law of Christ" refer? (See John 13:34; Galatians 5:14; and James 2:8 for further clarification.)

_____

_____

_____

What attitude does verse 3 discourage, and how will avoiding that attitude help us when we are seeking to restore another individual?

_____

_____

_____

If you had been overtaken by sin, how would you want someone to act toward you?

_____

_____

_____

When we see another believer who has been caught in the snare of sin, discerning love will act to help that individual overcome the sin and gain victory. Regrettably, Christians too often react in one or more of the following inappropriate ways:

- Ignoring the sin
- Harshly attacking the sinner instead of the sin
- Looking down on the individual
- Gossiping about the person
- Making no attempt to bring the individual to repentance and restoration

In this passage, Paul urges the Galatians to be tender yet firm—to forgive and help the sinner while confronting the sin. He urges them to be compassionate and not haughty in dealing with others. We must keep in mind that we are also prone to sin, and we cannot think of ourselves as better than the one we are trying to help. Recognizing our own susceptibility to sin will help keep us gentle and humble as we seek to help others.

Read 2 Corinthians 10:12 and Galatians 6:4-5. What does verse 4 encourage each person to do for himself or herself?

_____

_____

_____

How will testing your own actions help you as you seek to restore others?

_____

_____

_____

What action is discouraged?

_____

_____

_____

Why is comparing ourselves to others unwise?

_____

_____

_____

What does verse 5 indicate regarding each person's responsibility?

_____

_____

_____

_____

Before we can really help another individual, it is important that we examine our own lives and test our own actions. We need to ask ourselves, *Are my actions godly and my motives pure?* If we cannot honestly say yes, then we need to ask God to purify our actions and our motives or we will not be able to restore others.

Comparisons are also detrimental in our efforts to help others. When we compare ourselves to others, the usual results are either feelings of inferiority or feelings of prideful superiority. Both of these attitudes are destructive, and Paul prudently warns that those who "compare themselves with themselves . . . are not wise" (2 Corinthians 10:12).

When Paul urged the spiritually mature to help carry the "burdens" of others (verse 2), he was speaking of a load that is too heavy for one individual to carry. The Greek word for "burden" in verse 2 is different from the word used for "load" in verse 5. The word in verse 5 refers to a smaller load and implies a task or a service. Each individual should be encouraged to do his or her part; but when a person is facing a burden too heavy to carry, Christians need to lovingly step in to help carry that load, which may involve working to gently restore another believer who has slipped into sin.

According to 2 Timothy 2:25-26, how are God's servants encouraged to act toward those who oppose them?

_____

_____

_____

_____

What is the goal of gently instructing the opposing individual?

_____

_____

_____

_____

What do these verses imply about the manner in which genuine love confronts?

_____

_____

_____

Discerning love is careful in the manner in which it attempts correction and confrontation. Bullying others into repentance seldom brings lasting results. Gentle instruction and the truth spoken in love (see Ephesians 4:15) are far more effective in achieving the desired repentance and restoration.

A Closer Look at My Own Heart

Read Philippians 1:8-11 from several different translations. How does the apostle Paul describe his love for the Philippians (see verse 8)?

_____

_____

_____

What did Paul's love lead him to do for the Philippians?

_____

_____

_____

What did Paul pray for them in regard to their love (see verse 9)?

_____

_____

_____

The Greek word translated as "depth of insight" in the _New International Version_ can also be properly translated as "discernment" in the _Modern Language Bible_, the _New American Standard Bible_, the _New King James Version_ and the _Revised Standard Version_. What does it mean to you personally to have a love that abounds in knowledge and depth of insight or discernment?

_____

_____

_____

Love without guidelines and boundaries is not a healthy love, and is not the way God wants us to love. *Tolerating abuse, enabling addictions or condoning deliberate sin is not in the best interest of the other person.* As Paul prayed that the Philippians would "abound still more and more in real knowledge and all discernment" (Philippians 1:9, *NASB*), he identified these two qualities as essential to healthy love.

What is the result of love that abounds with knowledge and discernment?

_____

_____

_____

_____

As your love increases in knowledge and discernment, you will be able to recognize and approve what is best for your own life and also in your actions toward others. Your life will increasingly reflect Jesus' nature, and He will be glorified. Notice that Paul prays that their love will abound "more and more" in knowledge and discernment. This implies a growth process. Ask God to show you steps that you can take to help your love grow in knowledge and discernment. Record the ideas that God reveals to you.

_____

_____

_____

_____

_____

There will be times when you do not know how to best love another individual. Just as prayer was needed to help the Philippians grow in loving discernment, seeking God's guidance in prayer is essential to knowing how to love with a healthy love. Studying and knowing God's Word is another key to growing in wisdom and discernment. Sometimes you may also need to seek the objective advice of a godly counselor who can help you recognize unhealthy patterns and lead you to grow in discerning love.

According to James 1:5, what do you need to do when you lack wisdom?

_____

_____

_____

What is promised to those who ask in faith for God's wisdom?

_____

_____

_____

How does this promise apply to you and the areas where you need discernment in your love?

_____

_____

_____

Action Steps I Can Take Today

In what ways have you shown love in the past week? In your journal, list the different ways you have shown love to others. Evaluate those actions in regard to knowledge and discernment and answer the following questions:

- Have my actions helped the other individual grow?
- Have my actions in any way hindered God's work in his or her life?
- Have I done for others what they needed to do for themselves?
- Have my actions enabled others to continue in sin or in irresponsible behavior?
- Have I spoken the truth in love?
- Have my actions eliminated consequences that might have brought repentance?
- Have my actions been aimed at trying to bring restoration?

Ask God to show you any areas in which your actions of love may be enabling another individual to continue in sin; then record in your journal the insights God reveals to you.

Ask God to reveal where your love needs to grow in knowledge and be more discerning. Then ask God for a plan to help you grow in knowledge and discernment. Remember, God promises wisdom to those who ask for it (see James 1:5). In your journal, record the areas where you need to grow, along with the plan God gives to help you grow.

Pray Philippians 1:9-11 daily. On an index card, write a paraphrase of Paul's prayer for the Philippians, personalizing it and making it a prayer to God for yourself. Keep the card in your Bible and pray this prayer every day this week and whenever you feel a need for greater discernment in your love.

EIGHT

LOVE COVERS OVER WRONGS AND IS PATIENT

Sandi did not want her marriage to continue; she had been hurt too many times. As she reflected on past emotional wounds, her husband's faults seemed to grow in magnitude and importance, and she lost all hope of ever having a healthy marriage. Besides, her feelings of love were gone and she was ready to end the marriage and get on with her life. She had lost patience and hope, and, quite simply, no longer cared.

A Closer Look at the Problem

With the divorce rates soaring to unprecedented levels, is there any hope for a marriage like the one described above? Some people wonder if it is even possible to build enduring love into a relationship. When love has seemingly died, is there any way to revitalize the feelings that originally drew the individuals together?

As you study this chapter, you will see that God loves us with a patient and enduring love that does not magnify our sin, but covers over it with the blood of Jesus. He is in the business of restoring lives, restoring relationships and restoring marriages. Yes, through Jesus there is hope for troubled relationships. Love can be rekindled and revitalized, and sick relationships can be brought to health. Here is the threefold focus of this chapter:

1. To see how God loves you with an enduring love that covers your sin.
2. To understand how love covers over wrongs.
3. To learn how to build enduring love and renewed hope into relationships.

Before you begin your study, ask God to help you discern areas where your love needs to cover over wrongs; then give Him permission to change you. Will you ask Him to rekindle hope and love in relationships where you have been tempted to give up?

A Closer Look at God's Truth

Which phrase in 1 Peter 4:8 shows the importance of love?

_____

_____

_____

What action of love is described in this verse?

_____

_____

_____

What is meant by the phrase, "love covers over a multitude of sins"?

_____

_____

_____

How and why do you think this happens?

_____

_____

_____

In chapter 7, you learned that discerning love must sometimes confront sin in order to bring repentance and restoration. It is also important to recognize that discerning love is balanced and knows when to confront and when to overlook an offense. Every individual has weaknesses, and we all sin. Hatred causes us to see every flaw, expose and magnify weaknesses and be quick to gossip and complain. By contrast, love helps us overlook minor flaws and weaknesses, seek to protect and not draw attention to the character flaws of the loved individual.

According to 2 Corinthians 5:14-21, for whom did Christ die?

_____

_____

_____

What else has God, through Christ, done for us (see verses 18-19)?

_____

_____

_____

What did Christ become for us and what is the result for us (see verse 21)?

_____

_____

_____

What does the phrase "we might become the righteousness of God" (verse 21) mean to you?

_____

_____

_____

Which phrases in Isaiah 61:10 indicate that God's love covers over sin?

_____

_____

_____

When Jesus died on the cross, He paid the penalty for our sin by becoming sin for us; and in exchange, He gave us His righteousness. When God looks at a believer, He looks at that individual through the blood of Jesus, and He sees that believer as righteous. Through the sacrifice of Jesus, God's love has covered over and forgiven our sin. Accepting His love and forgiveness toward us helps us to accept ourselves and enables us to reach out with His love toward others.

What does it mean to you personally to be seen by God as righteous because of your faith in Jesus? Take a few minutes to ponder this blessing; then write a prayer of thanksgiving for His great love that covers over your sin.

_____

_____

_____

If you have never accepted Jesus as your Savior and Lord, will you choose to invite Him into your heart and life today? His love is eager and willing to cover the sin in your life and give you His righteousness. If you desire to receive Jesus, simply acknowledge that you are a sinner and ask Him to forgive you. Invite Him to come into your life and take control. He will graciously forgive and cover over your sin, and you will receive His righteousness. If you take this vital step, it is important that you share what you have done with another believer who can encourage you and rejoice with you.

The story of Noah and his three sons illustrates the difference between an action that exposes and love that covers over. According to Genesis 9:18-27, how did Ham respond to seeing his father naked and drunk?

_____

_____

_____

How did Shem and Japheth respond?

_____

_____

_____

What was the result of Ham's actions (see verses 24-25)?

_____

_____

_____

How were Shem and Japheth rewarded (see verses 26-27)?

_____

_____

_____

Even the righteous Noah had an obvious character flaw, and Ham saw the results. At that point, Ham had the choice of either covering his father or further exposing him. He chose to tell his brothers about their father's shameful condition. By contrast, Shem and Japheth chose to not look and to cover over their father's nakedness.

When we become aware of the character flaws of those around us, we also have choices. We can gossip and further expose the individual, or we can cover that person with love and prayers while seeking to help him or her overcome the character flaw.

It is important to note that Shem and Japheth were blessed because of their act of kindness, while Ham was cursed because of his actions. When we seek to expose another, we lose blessings and invite curses in the process.

What do the following verses reveal about love, gossip and malicious words?

Proverbs 10:12

_____
_____
_____

Proverbs 16:28

_____
_____
_____

Proverbs 26:20-22

_____
_____
_____

What does it show when you gossip about another?

_____
_____
_____

How is gossip the opposite of a love that covers over?

_____
_____
_____

What are some ways we can demonstrate a love that covers over sin?

_____
_____
_____

In marked contrast to a love that covers over sin is gossip that delights in *uncovering* and *exposing* the faults of others. The person who loves does not want to draw attention to the faults and shortcomings of the one he or she loves. While it may sometimes be necessary to expose and confront sin in order to bring restoration to the other individual, it is never done with pleasure or to hurt the individual and his or her reputation. *Love always seeks to help—never to hurt.*

In Titus 3:1-3, what instructions regarding our speech are found in verse 2?

_____

_____

_____

How is the unbeliever described (see verse 3)?

_____

_____

_____

In Titus 3:4-11, what attributes of God are given in verses 4 and 5?

_____

_____

_____

What actions in verses 4 through 7 demonstrate the love of God that covers over sin?

_____

_____

_____

_____

Why did God do these things for us?

_____

_____

_____

What should believers be careful to do, and why (see verse 8)?

_____

_____

_____

_____

What should they avoid, and why (see verse 9)?

_____

_____

_____

What does verse 11 tell about a person who causes division?

_____

_____

_____

How do gossip and foolish arguments contribute to divisions within a church or family?

_____

_____

_____

What can we do to prevent gossip and foolish arguments?

_____

_____

_____

If we are going to love as Jesus loves, we must refuse to allow ourselves to become part of gossip sessions. This means that we will not gossip, and we will not participate as listeners. The tales we hear go into our innermost being and become a part of the way we think of others. The more we gossip and complain about a person's faults, the worse he or she will appear to become. Although it may be necessary to confront an individual regarding sin in his or her life, exposing the faults of another through gossip is *never* a loving action. Ask God to give you discernment to recognize when it is in the best interest of another individual to cover over his or her sin, and when confrontation is necessary. Before taking action, ask yourself, *What is truly in the best interest of this individual?*

In Psalm 32:1-5, how does David describe the individual whose sins are covered (see verses 1-2)?

_____

_____

_____

How do these verses demonstrate the difference between love that covers over sin (see verses 1-2) and the attempt to cover up sin (see verses 3-5)?

_____

_____

_____

_____

How does David contrast the emotional effects of love that covers over sin with his attempt to cover up sin?

_____

_____

_____

It is important to recognize that love that covers over sin is not the same as an unhealthy attempt to *cover up* sin. In Psalm 32, David describes the intense agony that he felt while trying to cover up his adultery with Bathsheba and the murder of her husband, Uriah (see 2 Samuel 11-12). The purpose of the cover-up was to deceive, and God was displeased. In love, God sent the prophet Nathan to confront David.

Love that covers over sin recognizes and acknowledges the sin yet continues to love while seeking to bring healing and restoration. Discerning love addresses the sin and will confront when needed, but seeks to help the loved one overcome the sin. *Love that covers over can love the sinner without condoning the sin.* It looks at the sinner's shortcomings through love that covers over the sin with the healing balm of mercy and forgiveness, always seeking restoration. Covering up or denying abuse, deliberate sin or addictive behavior will not bring the healing and restoration we desire and should not be confused with love that covers over sin with mercy and forgiveness (see chapter 7 for further study of discerning love). In contrast to the healing potential of love that covers over sin, covering up deliberate sin is like applying a bandage to a dirty wound. Instead of getting healed, the wound is likely to become infected and create long-term problems.

Which phrases in 1 Corinthians 13:4-7 relate to gossip or love that covers over wrong?

_____

_____

_____

Which phrases speak of patience as an action of love?

_____

_____

_____

According to James 5:7-11, how long are we encouraged to be patient?

_____

_____

_____

What three examples of patience are given in this passage?

_____

_____

_____

_____

How does this passage define patience?

_____

_____

_____

_____

How is a farmer an example of patience?

_____

_____

_____

_____

How are Job and the prophets examples of patience?

_____

_____

_____

_____

What is encouraged in verse 8, and why?

_____

_____

_____

What action contrary to patience are we to avoid, and why?

_____

_____

_____

Why were the prophets regarded as happy or blessed (see verse 11)?

_____

_____

_____

In Job 42:10-17, how did God reward Job's patience?

_____

_____

_____

We often think that being patient means that we will never lose our temper. While patience will often help us to control our anger, the passage from James 5 defines patience as endurance or perseverance. Remaining in a difficult marriage or in any other unfulfilling relationship is not easy. Many people are quick to leave a marriage that they find does not meet their needs, and it seems easier to leave a church or dissolve a friendship than it is to work on correcting problems. While God does not expect us to live in dangerous and abusive situations, His kind of love does not easily give up. *Agape* love that always seeks the highest good for the other individual will seek a resolution to the difficulties whenever possible.

A Closer Look at My Own Heart

There are times when discouragement threatens to overwhelm, and the desire to give up on a relationship can be very strong. The remaining Scripture passages of this chapter contain promises that can help bring hope when you are struggling with discouragement. As you study these promises, apply them to your own situation. Remember that God's love for you is a love that does not give up, and He will help you build that same kind of love into your life if you sincerely seek His help.

Read the following verses and personalize the promises found in each, applying them to your own relationships:

Proverbs 16:7

_____

_____

_____

Proverbs 21:21

_____

_____

_____

Hebrews 4:14-16

_____

_____

_____

Which promise from these verses is most meaningful to you, and why? Memorize and personalize that promise. Write it on an index card and place it where you will see it often and be reminded this is God's promise to you.

Read Galatians 6:7-10. What are the warnings found in verse 7?

_____

_____

_____

What spiritual truths illustrated by nature are expressed in verses 7 and 8?

_____

_____

_____

How can these truths be a warning?

_____

_____

_____

How can they be a promise?

_____

_____

_____

How can verses 7 and 8 relate to loving others?

_____

_____

_____

_____

Ask God to show you "seeds," or actions, of love that you can sow into the life of another. List the actions that God brings to your mind.

_____

_____

_____

_____

_____

What does verse 9 urge you to avoid?

_____

_____

_____

What promise is given?

_____

_____

_____

_____

What is the condition for reaping the harvest?

_____

_____

_____

_____

What does verse 10 encourage you to do?

_____

_____

_____

The principle of sowing and reaping illustrates several spiritual truths that can be applied to loving others. We will reap what we sow. If we sow seeds of love, love will grow in our own lives and our relationships will become more loving. If we sow seeds of bitterness, discord or resentment, we can only expect the same in return.

We will reap in proportion to the amount that we sow. If we are stingy in the actions of love we give out, the love that comes back to us will be small. If we choose to love abundantly and freely, our harvest of love will be ample.

Seeds that are planted need time to grow. They must be watered and nurtured until they produce a harvest. To quit watering during a dry spell would greatly reduce the possibility of a good harvest. If our loving actions do not produce immediate results, we are often tempted to give up. If we want results, we must give the seeds time to grow.

In these verses, the apostle Paul urged the Galatians to refuse to give up and to keep sowing the good seeds that will bring forth a godly harvest. So keep sowing seeds of love. Claim God's promise that you will reap a harvest if you do not give up. With God's help, you can continue to nurture those seeds of love until they bring forth a harvest of love.

What does Paul request in his prayer in 1 Thessalonians 3:12-13?

_____

_____

_____

_____

What would be the result?

_____

_____

_____

_____

Action Steps I Can Take Today

Paraphrase the words of 1 Thessalonians 3:12-13 into your own personal prayer to God. Record this prayer in your journal and on an index card. Place it where you will see it often and be reminded to pray it regularly.

Evaluate your life in regard to your willingness to cover over sin. Ask God to make you aware of any areas in which you need to cover another's sin with mercy and forgiveness. Ask Him to help you discern between godly love that covers over sin and unhealthy love that seeks to deceive by covering up deliberate sin and abusive actions. Record in your journal what God reveals to you.

Evaluate your speech for gossip. Ask God to reveal to you any areas where you may be falling into gossip or using words to tear down others. Gossip can be carefully disguised as "Christian concern" or "prayer requests." If we are not a part of the problem or a part of the solution, we should not encourage gossip by listening. Record in your journal what God reveals to you.

Carefully monitor what comes out of your mouth. Before speaking, ask yourself the following:

- Is what I am saying true?
- Is it necessary?
- Is it kind?
- Will it build up or tear down?

Evaluate your level of love by reviewing the different actions of love you've studied in this book. Ask God to show you which actions of love are most needed in your own life. Will you ask for God's help in devising a plan to add those actions to your life? Record in your journal the plan of action God reveals to you. Share with another believer what God is revealing, and ask that individual to help you by praying for and with you and by checking your progress in the future.

Do not hesitate to seek help from a godly Christian counselor if you need further help in building love into your life. Sometimes we need the help of a godly professional trained in biblical counseling to help us overcome some of the stumbling blocks to love. The sooner you get help, the quicker you will begin to grow.

Allow God's love to empower you to love others. Never forget that God loves and values you immensely. He is always available to help you learn to walk in love and victory. As you seek His face and draw into His presence, His love in you will enable you to love others.

May the Lord make your love increase and overflow for each other and for everyone else, just as ours does for you. May he strengthen your hearts so that you will be blameless and holy in the presence of our God and Father when our Lord Jesus comes with all his holy ones (1 Thessalonians 3:12-13).

LOVING LIKE JESUS
LEADER'S GUIDE

The purpose of this leader's guide is to provide those willing to lead a group Bible study with additional material to make the study more effective. Each lesson has one or two exercises designed to increase participation and lead the group members into closer relationship with their heavenly Father.

The exercises are designed to introduce the study and emphasize the theme of the chapter. When two exercises are suggested, it is up to your discretion whether to use them both. Time will probably be the deciding factor.

If the group is larger than six members, you may want to break into smaller groups for the personal sharing time so that all will have an adequate opportunity to share. As the lessons proceed, the exercises will invite more personal sharing. Keep these two important points in mind:

1. Involve each member of the group in the discussion when at all possible. Some may be too shy or new to the Bible study experience. Be sensitive to their needs and encourage them to answer simple questions that do not require personal information or biblical knowledge. As they get more comfortable in the group, they will probably share more often.

2. Make a commitment with the group members that what is shared in the discussion times and prayer requests must be kept in strictest confidence.

After each lesson, be prepared to pray with those who have special needs or concerns. Emphasize the truth of God's Word as you minister to the group members, leading them to a closer relationship with their Lord and Savior.

ONE

*L*OVE IS IMPORTANT

Objective

To help group members understand how important it is to their relationship with God that they exhibit Christlike love with everyone.

Preparation

EXERCISE 1

Obtain a whiteboard, chalkboard or flipchart and felt-tip pens or chalk.

EXERCISE 2

Obtain four large 12 x 18-inch sheets of construction paper or poster board, a pad of sticky notes (or several small pieces of plain paper), masking or transparent tape and pens or pencils. Using a felt-tip pen, write one of each of the following words in large letters across the top of a separate sheet of the construction paper (or poster board): "heart," "mind," "soul" and "strength."

DISCUSSION

Familiarize yourself with the questions in the following Group Participation section, and choose which questions you definitely want to discuss with the group. Note that there might not be time to discuss every question, so modify or adapt this discussion guide to fit the needs of your group. Additional discussion questions/action steps are provided to stimulate further discussion if you have the time. If you haven't already done so for exercise 1, obtain a whiteboard, chalkboard or flipchart and felt-tip pens or chalk.

Group Participation

EXERCISE 1

Invite group members to share ways God shows love to them each day. As they share, write their responses on the whiteboard, chalkboard or flipchart. After a couple of minutes of sharing, ask group members to brain-storm ways that they can share the ways that God loves them with others. For example, someone might say that God shows His grace by forgiving us when we sin. The way we can show that same grace to others is to forgive them when they sin against us.

EXERCISE 2

Read Luke 10:25-28. Review with group members what "heart," soul," "mind" and "strength" mean in the context of these verses. Invite group members to share one example of how we can love God with each aspect of our being. Discuss which of the ways of loving God are easiest and which are more difficult. Give each group member four pieces of sticky notes or small pieces of paper and have them write how they will show their love for God in each of these four aspects. Give them a couple of min-utes, and then invite them to stick their notes to the appropriate sheet of paper. Keep these sheets of paper for future reference during the course of this study. Continue to remind members of what they have written dur-ing following sessions.

DISCUSSION

1. Discuss the following questions (or the ones you have chosen) from the "A Closer Look at God's Truth" section:

    *   In Matthew 22:34-30, why did Jesus give two commands in-stead of one when the Pharisee asked for the single most important commandment? How does Jesus relate these two commandments to the Law and the prophets?
    *   According to Romans 13:8-10, what debt do we always owe to others? How does obeying the commandment to love fulfill the Law?
    *   What does it mean to you to love God with all your heart, soul, strength and mind? What does loving your neighbor as yourself involve?
    *   How does loving God relate to salvation and trusting in God? How does loving others relate to your salvation?
    *   In Luke 10:29-37, when the expert asked Jesus a question, why did Jesus answer with a parable? Why did the priest and Levite in the parable go by the man without stopping?

- Why do you think love is important if we are to live a victorious life in Christ?

2. Discuss the following questions (or the ones you have chosen) from the "A Closer Look at My Own Heart" section:

   - What actions of love does Jesus ask us to perform in Luke 6:27-28? How do you think obeying these commands would affect your feelings?
   - What practical action of love is found in Luke 6:31? What are some practical ways that you could apply this to your relationships?
   - What actions of love are commanded in Romans 12:17-21? How do these instructions relate to the actions in Luke 6?
   - In Luke 6:32-36, what actions did Jesus describe that even sinners do? Why are Christians to be different in this regard?
   - What will be the results of following Jesus' instructions?

ADDITIONAL DISCUSSION/ACTION STEPS

1. Discuss how our busyness can hinder our ability to love God. What are some other hindrances to loving Him?

2. Discuss how our lack of love hurts our effectiveness as Christ's representatives to the world. What could we do if we observe another Christian behaving in an unloving way?

3. Discuss how memorizing Scripture can help us learn to love God with all our heart, soul, mind and strength. Challenge members to memorize one Scripture verse each week during this study. Suggest that they begin with Luke 10:27. Invite group members to share if they regularly memorize Scripture and how that has affected their relationship with God.

4. Invite members to find an accountability partner within the group and ask each group member to share with their partner one tangible way each of them will show love to God during the week. Have the partners trade phone numbers or email addresses and contact one another during the week to encourage one another in loving God.

TWO

ℒOVE IS POWERFUL

Objective

To help group members understand the power of God's love to change their own lives and the lives of others as they put His love into action.

Preparation

EXERCISE 1

If your group is new to the practice of journaling, obtain an inexpensive journal and a pen for each group member. Prepare to share how journaling has helped you in your spiritual journey.

EXERCISE 2

Cut nine circles (approximately 6 to 8 inches in diameter) out of purple or green paper (these will be used to represent grapes in a cluster). Using a felt-tip pen, label each circle with one aspect of the fruit of the Spirit listed in Galatians 5:22-23: "love," "joy," "peace," "patience," "kindness," "goodness," "faithfulness," "gentleness" and "self-control." Obtain a large sheet of poster board and masking or transparent tape. On the poster board, roughly sketch a thick vine across the top of the poster and write the words "I am the vine; you are the branches" inside the vine. Across the bottom write, "The Fruit of the Spirit." Display the poster in the meeting room.

DISCUSSION

Familiarize yourself with the questions in the following Group Participation section and in the lesson, and choose which questions you definitely want to discuss with the group. Obtain a whiteboard, chalkboard or flipchart and felt-tip pens or chalk.

Group Participation

EXERCISE 1

Share how journaling has helped you along your road to spiritual maturity, and invite other group members to share how journaling has helped them grow in their relationship with the Lord. Give each group member a journal and a pen, and challenge them to begin (or continue) this practice. Encourage them to write responses, prayers, challenges and goals regarding each week's lesson during the course of this study. Refer to the directions in this week's lesson to write about the verses regarding their prayer lives. If they haven't already done so, give them a few moments right now to respond in their journals.

EXERCISE 2
Hand out one of the "grapes" with a piece of tape attached to it to the first nine people who arrive. (For a smaller group, you will have to give some people more than one.) Invite a volunteer to read Galatians 5:13-14,22-23,25 and another to read John 15:5-12. Discuss how these two Scripture passages are related. Point out that the attributes described in Galatians 5:22-23 are called the "fruit" of the Spirit—not separate fruits, but one fruit. These are not like the gifts of the Spirit, where each believer may have different ones. Emphasize that every believer must display the *whole fruit*.

Ask the volunteer who read the Galatians passage to read verses 22-23 slowly. As each fruit is mentioned, have the person who has that "grape" attach it to the poster, helping them arrange the papers like a bunch of grapes, but so that each attribute can be read. If you have time, discuss what each attribute means. Encourage members to memorize this verse to aid them in developing the fruit of the Spirit in their lives.

DISCUSSION
1. Discuss the following questions (or the ones you have chosen) from the "A Closer Look at God's Truth" section:

   • According to Colossians 2:2-3, what was Paul's twofold intention for ministry to these people? What did he hope would be the result of the encouragement and unity?
   • What phrases from Jesus' prayer in John 17:20-23 suggest Christians are to be united and loving toward each other?
   • What tragic result of division is described in Luke 11:17? How does this apply to a home? How does this apply to a fellowship?
   • What do you think is meant by 1 John 3:17? How do our words express love?

- What is promised in 1 John 3:21-24? What commands must we obey to receive these promises?
- What does 1 John 4:7 tell us about the person who "has been born of God"? What does it mean to be born of God?

2. Discuss the following questions (or the ones you have chosen) from the "A Closer Look at My Own Heart" section:

- What does it mean to "remain," or abide, in Jesus? What is promised to the one who remains or abides in Jesus?
- According to John 15:14-6, what are the results of not remaining in Jesus?
- What result of the Spirit-filled life is described in Romans 5:5?
- How do the truths recorded in 2 Corinthians 3:17-18 relate to our ability to love?
- Do you need to make any changes in your attitude or actions to be able to claim that promise?

ADDITIONAL DISCUSSION/ACTION STEPS

1. Discuss the relationship between love and unity in the Church. What thoughts, attitudes and actions contribute to disunity in the Church? What can we do to show God's love to other believers?

2. Invite volunteers to share ways they have experienced God's love through the words and actions of other believers. If no one volunteers, prepare to share your own experience. Ask if anyone has especially experienced the *power* of God's love in their lives or seen it in the lives of others.

3. Invite volunteers to share if they were able to carry out last week's challenge to love God with all their hearts, souls, minds and strength. Ask them to share any insights they received during the week. Continue to remind members of this challenge each week.

4. Close the meeting in prayer, inviting group members to pray silently regarding the fruit of the Spirit they need to cultivate in their lives.

THREE

Love is Accepting

Objective

To help group members understand the loving acceptance that God has demonstrated toward each of them and learn how to extend that loving acceptance to others who are difficult to love.

Preparation

Exercise 1

Obtain pens or pencils and enough index cards for each group member to have at least one.

Exercise 2

Obtain a whiteboard, chalkboard or flipchart and felt-tip pens or chalk.

Discussion

Familiarize yourself with the questions in the following Group Participation section and in the lesson, and choose which questions you definitely want to discuss with the group.

Group Participation

Exercise 1

As group members arrive, give each person an index card and a pen or pencil. Once everyone is settled, discuss in what ways Jesus demonstrated His loving acceptance for us. After a few minutes of discussion, invite members to write one way that they have experienced God's loving acceptance—it could be through something they have read in God's Word or something someone has said or done for them.

Once they have completed their writing, ask them to turn the card over and write the name of one person in their life whom they need to accept.

Next to the name, ask them to write a specific action they will take in the next week to demonstrate that kind of love to the person. Instruct them to put the card in their study book at the beginning of next week's lesson. Be sure to ask them to share any results at next week's session.

EXERCISE 2

Ask a volunteer to read 1 John 3:1 in the *New International Version*. Ask group members to share what word pictures or synonyms the word "lavish" brings to mind. Write their synonyms on the board or chart. Share that according to *Merriam-Webster's Collegiate Dictionary* "prodigal" is one listed synonym for the adjective "lavish," and "squander" is a synonym for the verb form of "lavish." Discuss how this information affects their understanding of God's lavish love for us in relation to the story of the prodigal son found in Luke 15:11-24.

DISCUSSION

1. Discuss the following questions (or the ones you have chosen) from the "A Closer Look at God's Truth" section:

    *   In John 13:34-35, how did Jesus command His disciples to love? What would be the result of that kind of love?

    *   According to Romans 5:8, how is the love of God demonstrated? What phrase implies that Jesus' love is accepting?

    *   According to Luke 15:11-24, what were the actions of the younger son that would make it difficult to accept him? Why did he decide to return to his father? What emotions do you think the son felt as he drew close to home?

    *   In Luke 15:25-32, how did the older brother react to his brother's return? What was his focus?

    *   What are we commanded to do in Romans 14:1? Why are we commanded to accept others without judgment?

    *   According to Romans 14:13, what attitudes do we need to demonstrate toward persons whose actions are different from ours?

    *   What does Romans 15:7 command us to do, and what will be the result? What does it mean to you to "accept one another . . . as Christ accepted you"?

2. Discuss the following questions (or the ones you have chosen) from the "A Closer Look at My Own Heart" section:

    • What does Luke 6:41-42 teach us about condemning others?
    • What important truth concerning our words and actions is found in Luke 6:45?
    • According to Philippians 4:8, what should be the focus of your mind?

ADDITIONAL DISCUSSION/ACTION STEPS

1. Invite volunteers to share about a time they were recipients of the loving acceptance of another believer.

2. Discuss who the older brother in the prodigal son parable might represent. Discuss how long-time believers sometimes might behave like the older son.

3. Invite volunteers to share any results of the action steps they might have taken as a result of this lesson.

4. Continue to encourage and challenge group members to memorize Scripture and write in their journals.

$\mathscr{L}$OVE IS FORGIVING

Objective

To help group members fully experience God's forgiveness and extend that forgiveness to others.

Preparation

EXERCISE 1

Prepare a cross made out of two 2x4-inch pieces of lumber and "plant" it in a pot filled with dirt. Obtain small nails and hammers. Also prepare small slips of paper approximately 2x2-inches square and obtain pens or pencils. Obtain a CD of worship music and a player. Provide a document shredder. (As an option, you could also draw a simple cross on a large sheet of butcher paper and provide sticky notes or slips of paper with transparent tape and pens or pencils. Hang the cross on a wall of the meeting room.)

EXERCISE 2

You will use the cross that you have prepared for this exercise as well. This exercise could be used as a concluding activity for this session.

DISCUSSION

Familiarize yourself with the questions in the following Group Participation section and in the lesson, and choose which questions you definitely want to discuss with the group. Obtain a whiteboard, chalkboard or flipchart and felt-tip pens or chalk. (Note: This lesson may bring up strong emotions in some group members. Be prepared to pray with any members who have specific concerns about forgiveness and anger.)

Group Participation

EXERCISE 1

Read Ephesians 1:4,7 and discuss what Christ did for us on the cross. Share Romans 5:8 and discuss for what Christ died. Give each member a slip of paper and a pen or pencil, and then read 1 John 1:9. Invite group members to prayerfully consider at least one sin that they have struggled to break in their lives and write it on the paper. Ask them to fold the paper in half and attach it to the cross while you play the worship music,

Spend some time in silent prayer after everyone has completed the task. Tell members that these slips of paper will be destroyed and that not even you will read them—*and then keep that promise!* If possible, at the end of the meeting shred the slips of paper without unfolding them. Remind the group members that that is what happens to the sins for which we have asked the Lord's forgiveness—they are forgotten.

EXERCISE 2
At the end of the meeting, invite the group members to write down the name of someone they need to forgive or someone from whom they need to ask forgiveness. Attach these papers to the cross you have prepared. Invite any members who would like you to personally pray for them to stay after the meeting.

DISCUSSION
1. Discuss the following questions (or the ones you have chosen) from the "A Closer Look at God's Truth" section:

    •   In Matthew 9:1-8, why do you think Jesus addressed the man's need for forgiveness before He healed him? What did the man's healing demonstrate?
    •   According to Luke 23:32-34, how did Jesus react to the mistreatment that He received? What effect do you think His forgiveness might have had on those who had mistreated Him?
    •   According to Colossians 3:12-14, what character qualities do God's people need to exhibit? What instructions are given regarding forgiveness?
    •   In Ephesians 4:26-27, what instructions does Paul give regarding anger? What sinful tendency in handling anger does Paul warn against?
    •   What guidelines regarding your speech does Paul give to us in Ephesians 5:29? How can those guidelines help you to resolve anger?

- How can inappropriate handling of anger grieve the Holy Spirit?

2. Discuss the following questions (or the ones you have chosen) from the "A Closer Look at My Own Heart" section:

   - In Matthew 18:21-22, how many times did Jesus say we should forgive?
   - In Matthew 18:23-27, how much did the first servant owe the king? How did the king respond to the servant's plea?
   - According to Matthew 18:28-35, how much did the fellow servant owe the first servant? How did he treat the man who owed him the relatively small sum of money?
   - What effect did this servant's lack of forgiveness have on the man who owed him?
   - How did this man's lack of forgiveness destroy him?
   - What consequence of not forgiving can be found in Matthew 18:35?

ADDITIONAL DISCUSSION/ACTION STEPS

1. Invite members to share any results they have seen of their assignment to show loving acceptance to another person during the last week.

2. Discuss in what situations it would not be advisable to express forgiveness in person to someone who has wronged them (for instance, in the case of abuse by a relative or being the victim or a crime). Discuss how to handle the need to forgive another in such a situation, such as by asking for godly counsel from a pastor, counselor or a spiritual mentor.

3. In some cases, we have to ask forgiveness of someone who is not available for us to approach in person (for instance, someone who has died or someone with whom we have lost contact). Invite members to suggest what could be done to help a person ask for forgiveness in such a situation.

4. Discuss how, despite the cruelties Jesus experienced before and during His crucifixion, He was still able to pray, "Father, forgive them for

they do not know what they are doing" (Luke 23:34). Challenge members to remember this verse whenever they are having difficulty forgiving those who have hurt them. Remind them that forgiving others is an ongoing struggle. It will only be through the power of the Holy Spirit living in them and their relationship with the Lord that they will be able to forgive those who hurt them.

5. If you do not do exercise 2 as a conclusion, spend some time in prayer for group members to have the strength to forgive and ask for forgiveness. Be available after the meeting to pray with individuals who are struggling with their own forgiveness from God, their forgiveness of those who have hurt them, and their need to seek forgiveness of those whom they have wronged.

*L*OVE IS SACRIFICING AND SERVING

Objective

To help group members see the sacrificial love of Jesus and to help them take on the challenge of doing specific acts of serving others with the love of Christ.

Preparation

EXERCISE 1

Prepare to do a foot-washing service with group members. You will need one plastic dishpan for approximately every four to five group members, a towel for every member, plastic pitchers, a mild soap (such as Ivory®), large tubs or a nearby sink to provide water, and a place to throw out used water. You could ask group members to supply some of these items.

If you plan on doing this exercise, you might want to contact group members ahead of time so they can wear appropriate clothing. In addition, some members may want to opt out for various reasons. If they do, ask them to perform another job such as emptying or filling dishpans, providing dry towels, and so forth. You will need to enlist the help of a few of the group members to assist you. (Optional: Obtain a worship CD and CD player or a digital media player.)

Set up the meeting room (or a separate room) with chairs arranged in a circle. If you have a large group, arrange several smaller circles. If you do not have easy access to a sink, you will need to have water provided in large tubs for dispensing water and then empty tubs to throw out the used water.

EXERCISE 2

Obtain a whiteboard, chalkboard or flipchart and felt-tip pens or chalk.

DISCUSSION

Familiarize yourself with the questions in the following Group Participation section and in the lesson, and choose which questions you definitely want to discuss with the group.

Group Participation

EXERCISE 1

Read John 13:1-17. Remind members that in Jesus' day, it was commonly the dinner host's responsibility to see that his guests' feet were washed, and this act was usually done by one of the lowliest servants in the household. Ask the members to imagine the scene in their minds. Demonstrate how to do the foot-washing by washing the feet of the first person in the circle.

When you have washed that person's feet, he or she will wash the next person's feet. Having someone else there to empty the dishpan and another to fill it with fresh water will help move this activity along. You may want to play worship music while the foot-washing is taking place, or encourage the members to sing as they wash each other's feet. When you are done, discuss the experience:

- What were your thoughts while your feet were being washed? What were your thoughts as you were washing another member's feet?

- What thoughts do you suppose were going through the disciples' minds as Jesus was washing their feet?

- Why is this action of Jesus so amazing? How does it affect your thoughts on loving others sacrificially?

EXERCISE 2

Invite group members to share practical ways they can show love to others in the church, in the community, in their families, to their enemies, and in other parts of the world. Write the ideas on the whiteboard, chalkboard or flipchart. Discuss which idea(s) the group could do to show love to others, and challenge them to carry through on at least one idea. Make specific plans with the whole group to do an act of sacrificial service together during the week.

DISCUSSION

1. Discuss the following questions (or the ones you have chosen) from the "A Closer Look at God's Truth" section:

   - In John 15:9-15, what does Jesus promise those who keep His commands? What did Jesus command us to do?
   - According to 1 John 4:9-12, how did God show His love for us? What should be the result of receiving God's great love for us?
   - What instructions are given in Ephesians 5:1? What does it mean to imitate God as His "dearly loved children"?
   - What did Jesus' washing of the disciples' feet in John 13:1-5 show? How did His willingness to become a servant relate to His greatness?
   - What instructions did Jesus give in John 13:14-15? What promise is given for those who obey these instructions?
   - How does Galatians 5:13 instruct us regarding our use of freedom and its relationship to love?

2. Discuss the following questions (or the ones you have chosen) from the "A Closer Look at My Own Heart" section:

   - Which of the actions and attitudes listed in Philippians 2:1-11 are strengths for you? Which are weaknesses that point to areas of needed growth?
   - What qualities did Paul encourage when he urged the Philippians (and us) to have the same attitude Jesus had?
   - How does Philippians 2:1-11 relate to Paul's passage on the renewing of the mind in Romans 12:1-2?
   - How would your relationships be changed if you were to use Philippians 2:3-8 as your guide?
   - What changes do you need to make to put these verses into practice?

ADDITIONAL DISCUSSION/ACTION STEPS

1. Invite group members to share ways in which they have been blessed by the sacrificial love and service of others. Also ask them to share ways they have been blessed while serving others.

2. Discuss how sacrificial/servant love could make a difference in our relationships with others. Invite members to share ideas, and challenge each of them to commit to doing at least one act of sacrificial love for someone in their life during the next few weeks.

3. Instruct members to find an accountability partner within the group and ask each group member to share with their partner one tangible way each of them will show love to another during the week. Have the partners trade phone numbers or email addresses and contact one another during the week to encourage one another in sharing love.

SIX

ℒOVE IS KIND AND UPLIFTING

Objective

To help group members understand the power of positive words and kindness, which will bring glory to God and encouragement to others.

Preparation

EXERCISE

No preparation necessary.

DISCUSSION

Familiarize yourself with the questions in the following Group Participation section and in the lesson, and choose which questions you definitely want to discuss with the group.

Group Participation

EXERCISE

Invite members to share if they have done any acts of sacrificial love after last meeting's challenge. Ask what the results of serving others in love have been. Relate those acts of love to this session's lessons about being kind and uplifting. Continue to encourage one another in putting God's Word into action.

DISCUSSION

1. Discuss the following questions (or the ones you have chosen) from the "A Closer Look at God's Truth" section:

   • What actions are given in 1 Corinthians 13:4-7 that describe kindness? What are some of the ways in which you have personally benefited from God's lovingkindness toward you?

- Which phase in 2 Peter 1:5-9 indicates the individual's responsibility in Christian growth? What character qualities need to be added to faith?
- How does unkindness keep a Christian from being effective and productive? How can kindness increase your effectiveness?
- According to 2 Timothy 2:22-24, what kinds of arguments are you to avoid, and why? What is the difference between an argument and a quarrel? How can quarreling lead to unkindness and resentfulness?
- What qualities does 2 Timothy 2:24 say the Lord's servant should possess? Why is kindness so important if you are going to be an effective teacher?
- How do unkind actions bring disrespect to God? How does kindness bring God glory?
- According to 1 Corinthians 8:1, what does love do? How does that action relate to your words?

2. Discuss the following questions (or the ones you have chosen) from the "A Closer Look at My Own Heart" section:

- According to Ephesians 4:29-32, what kind of talk should not come out of your mouth?
- What should your words accomplish?
- When do your words grieve the Holy Spirit?

ADDITIONAL DISCUSSION/ACTION STEPS

1. Invite group members to briefly describe the kind acts of others that have had positive effects on them. Discuss how kindness helps God's teachings to have an effect on those who do not know Him.

2. Is it really true that "sticks and stones may break my bones, but words will never hurt me"? Invite members to share some examples of words that hurt more than physical injuries. How can we counteract the words that have hurt us? Besides asking for their forgiveness, what can we do to counteract the hurtful words we have spoken to others?

3. Discuss some examples of godless chatter that lead to ungodly actions. What can we do to avoid godless chatter or to turn it around to more edifying or encouraging words?

4. Discuss ways that we can encourage one another to be kinder and to use uplifting words as we respond to others throughout the day. Stress the importance of spending time with the Lord at the beginning and throughout the day to prepare our hearts, minds and tongues to speak in love and to be kind. Recite the suggested memory verse together (Psalm 19:14). Spend time in prayer, allowing group members to express their need to be more loving and kind.

$\mathscr{L}$OVE IS DISCERNING

Objective

To help group members understand that love must be discerning when dealing with someone who is continuing to sin and/or is harming others.

Preparation

EXERCISE 1

Prepare for a role-play activity by preparing several index cards with situations that require discerning love to help restore a sinner to a right relationship with the Lord. Some examples might include an unmarried daughter who is sleeping with her boyfriend, a Christian who has become an alcoholic, a Christian friend who loves to gossip, and so forth. Have enough situations so that groups of two or three can act out what they would do to confront the individual situation.

EXERCISE 2

Familiarize yourself with the story of David's sin with Bathsheba found in 2 Samuel 11 and with the prophet Nathan's rebuke of David in 2 Samuel 12.

DISCUSSION

Familiarize yourself with the questions in the following Group Participation section and in the lesson, and choose which questions you definitely want to discuss with the group.

Group Participation

EXERCISE 1

As members arrive, give a situation card to each group of two or three. Instruct them to read their situation, discuss what could be done, and then assign roles. After a few minutes, give each group the opportunity to act out their situation. (If time is limited, the group is too large or they might not participate in role-play, you could read two or three of the situations and have members respond to how they would act. Emphasize that the goal should be to restore the offender to a right relationship with the Lord.)

EXERCISE 2
Share the story of David's sin with Bathsheba and the resulting death of her husband, Uriah. Discuss the following:

- How did David get caught up in this sin?
- What were the results of his initial sin of sleeping with Bathsheba?
- How did he pile sin upon sin?
- Why do you suppose no one confronted or stopped him?

Read the account of Nathan's rebuke to David in 2 Samuel 12. Discuss the following:

- What technique did Nathan use to confront David about his sin?
- Why was Nathan's technique so effective with David?
- What were the consequences of David's sin?
- What were the consequences of his repentance? (Read Psalm 51 to demonstrate the effectiveness of Nathan's story in convicting David's heart of the sins he had committed.)

Point out that Nathan used a technique of drawing a word picture to help David understand the depth of his sin and affect him on an emotional level about the evil he had done. Encourage group members to try this technique in confronting someone whose actions are leading them into sin.

DISCUSSION
1. Discuss the following questions (or the ones you have chosen) from the "A Closer Look at God's Truth" section:

- What does Hebrews 12:5-6 teach us about God's love? How should we respond to God's discipline?
- What sin was Paul confronting in 1 Corinthians 5:1-6? What had been the attitude of the church? What attitudes should they have had?

- Which words in 2 Corinthians 7:2-4 express Paul's love for the Corinthians? How does he affirm them?
- According to 2 Corinthians 7:10-11, what is the difference between "worldly sorrow" and "godly sorrow"? What had the godly sorrow produced?
- In 2 Corinthians 2:4-11, what actions of love does Paul urge toward the sinning man in the Corinthian church? Why does he urge this?
- What does Paul mean in Galatians 6:1 when he says to "restore that person gently"? What caution should we take when seeking to restore another believer? Why is this important?
- What does Galatians 6:4 encourage each person to do for himself or herself? How will testing our own actions help us as we seek to restore others?

2. Discuss the following questions (or the ones you have chosen) from the "A Closer Look at My Own Heart" section:

- How does the apostle Paul describe his love for the believers in Philippians 1:8-11? What did Paul's love lead him to do for the Philippians?
- What is the result of love that abounds with knowledge and discernment?
- According to James 1:5, what do you need to do when you lack wisdom? What is promised to those who ask in faith for God's wisdom?

ADDITIONAL DISCUSSION/ACTION STEPS
1. Discuss why we are warned in Galatians 6:1-5 to be careful to examine our own actions when confronting someone about his or her sin.

2. Invite members to briefly share their experiences—both good and bad—with confronting others about their sin. Ask them to not give specifics or name names in order to protect the identities of those they have confronted. Ask if there are any brave souls who would be willing to share a time when another person lovingly confronted them on their sin.

3. Close by praying Paul's prayer in Philippians 1:9-11 together.

EIGHT

*L*OVE COVERS OVER WRONGS AND IS PATIENT

Objective

To help group members understand when and how to cover over the wrongs of others and to understand the role of being patient in love.

Preparation

EXERCISE 1
Obtain a whiteboard, chalkboard or flipchart, and felt-tip pens or chalk.

EXERCISE 2
Invite someone—preferably one of the group members—to lead the group in singing two or three praise and worship songs about God's love and mercy. Or obtain a worship CD and CD player or digital media player. This will be used at the end of the session.

DISCUSSION
Familiarize yourself with the questions in the following Group Participation section and in the lesson, and choose which questions you definitely want to discuss with the group. (Note: There might be group members who have accepted the Lord this week, as this week's study invited those who have not yet received Christ as Savior and Lord to do so. Provide an opportunity to allow them to make a public commitment. Approach this session with a lot of prayer. Also be prepared with follow-up materials and contacts.)

Group Participation

EXERCISE 1
Begin by discussing how last week's emphasis was on confronting others with a discerning love and this week's lesson is on covering over wrongs

and practicing patient love. Draw a line horizontally across the top of the board and then another line vertically down the center through the first line. Label one side of the horizontal line "sins to confront" and the other side "wrongs to cover." Invite group members to suggest actions that need to be confronted and corrected and actions that need to be covered with love. After you have a few listed on each side, discuss how a believer might deal with each situation listed.

DISCUSSION

1. Discuss the following questions (or the ones you have chosen) from the "A Closer Look at God's Truth" section:

    •   What is meant in 1 Peter 4:8 by the phrase, "love covers over a multitude of sins"? How and why do you think that this happens?
    •   According to Genesis 9:18-27, how did Ham respond to seeing his father naked and drunk? What was the result of Ham's actions? How were Shem and Japheth rewarded?
    •   How is gossip the opposite of a love that covers over? What are some ways we can demonstrate a love that covers over sin?
    •   What does Titus 3:11 tell about a person who causes division? How do gossip and foolish arguments contribute to division within a church or family?
    •   In Psalm 32:1-5, how does David describe the individual whose sins are covered? How does David contrast the emotional effects of love that covers over sin with his attempt to cover up sin?
    •   According to James 5:7-11, how long are we encouraged to be patient? How does James define patience?

2. Discuss the following questions (or the ones you have chosen) from the "A Closer Look at My Own Heart" section:

    •   What warnings are found in Galatians 6:7?
    •   What spiritual truths illustrated by nature does Paul express in Galatians 6:7-8? How can these verses relate to loving others?

- What does Galatians 6:9 urge us to avoid? What is the condition for reaping the harvest?
- What does Galatians 6:10 encourage us to do?

ADDITIONAL DISCUSSION/ACTION STEPS

1. Invite group members to share which of the promises from Proverbs 16:7; 21:21 or Hebrews 4:14-16 (from the "A Closer Look at My Own Heart" section) they found to be the most meaningful for their own life circumstances. Invite a few volunteers to read the personalized promises that they wrote.

2. Invite volunteers to share how they have seen the positive aspects of the principle of reaping what we sow in their own lives or the lives of others. Encourage them to speak honestly about persevering when they grow weary in doing good.

3. Ask how these principles of persevering in love can be applied in dealing with a difficult relationship with a loved one, such as an unfaithful spouse, a wandering child, a hurtful friend. Discuss when do we cover over wrongs done to us by another and when do we confront their actions as sin.

EXERCISE 2

Close this final session with a time of praise and worship, thanking God for His great love and mercy. Read 1 Thessalonians 3:12-13 in unison (found at the end of this session's lesson). Invite members to pray brief sentence prayers in response to the love of God that they have experienced during this study. Conclude with singing praise and worship songs about God's love and mercy.

(Note: Invite any new believers to stay after the meeting to discuss the life-changing step they have taken and what it means. Give them the materials you have collected. Also, extend the invitation to become a believer to the group members at the end of this session in case someone else is ready to make this commitment now.)

WHAT IS AGLOW INTERNATIONAL?

———◦○◦———

From one nation to 172 worldwide...
From one fellowship to more than 4,600...
From 100 people to more than 17 million...

———◦○◦———

Aglow International has experienced phenomenal growth since its inception more than 40 years ago. In 1967, four women from the state of Washington prayed for a way to reach out to other Christian women in simple fellowship, free from denominational boundaries.

———◦○◦———

The first meeting held in Seattle, Washington, USA, drew more than 100 women to a local hotel. From that modest beginning, Aglow International has become one of the largest intercultural, interdenominational Christian organizations in the world.

———◦○◦———

Each year, an estimated 17 million people are ministered to through Aglow's local fellowship meetings, Bible studies, support groups, retreats, conferences and various outreaches. From the inner city to the upper echelons, from the next door neighbor to the corporate executive, Aglow seeks to minister to the felt needs of women and men around the world.

———◦○◦———

Christian women and men find Aglow a "safe place" to grow spiritually and begin to discover and use the gifts, talents and abilities God has given them. Aglow offers excellent leadership training and varied opportunities to develop those leadership skills.

———◦○◦———

Undergirding the evangelistic thrust of the ministry is an emphasis on prayer, which has led to an active prayer network linking six continents. The vast prayer power available through Aglow women and men around the world is being used by God to influence countless lives in families, communities, cities and nations.

$\mathscr{A}$GLOW'S MISSION STATEMENT IS . . .

- To help restore and mobilize women and men around the world

- To promote gender reconciliation in the Body of Christ as God designed

- To amplify awareness of global concerns from a biblical perspective

---

$\mathscr{A}$GLOW'S THREE MANDATES

1. To promote gender reconciliation between male and female in the Body of Christ as God designed.

2. To answer God's call to minister to the Muslim people, while bringing awareness of the basic theological differences between Islam and Christianity.

3. To stand in loving support for Israel and the Jewish people, while helping to bring awareness to the Body of Christ concerning God's plans and purposes for those people He calls the "apple of His eye."

*A*GLOW MINISTERS IN . . .

Albania, Angola, Anguilla, Antigua, Argentina, Aruba, Australia, Austria, Bahamas, Bahrain, Barbados, Belarus, Belgium, Belize, Benin, Bermuda, Bolivia, Botswana, Brazil, Britain, Bulgaria, Burkina Faso, Cameroon, Canada, Chile, China, Colombia, Congo (Dem. Rep. of), Congo (Rep. of), Costa Rica, Côte d'Ivoire, Cuba, Curaçao, Czech Republic, Denmark, Djibouti, Dominica, Dominican Republic, Ecuador, Egypt, El Salvador, Equatorial Guinea, Estonia, Ethiopia, Faroe Islands, Fiji, Finland, France, Gabon, the Gambia, Germany, Ghana, Grand Cayman, Greece, Grenada, Guam, Guatemala, Guinea, Guyana, Haiti, Honduras, Hungary, Iceland, India, Indonesia, Ireland, Israel, Jamaica, Japan, Kenya, Korea, Kyrgyzstan, Latvia, Lithuania, Malawi, Malaysia, Mali, Mauritius, Mexico, Mongolia, Mozambique, Myanmar, Nepal, Netherlands, New Zealand, Nicaragua, Niger, Nigeria, Norway, Oman, Pakistan, Panama, Papua New Guinea, Peru, Philippines, Portugal, Puerto Rico, Romania, Russia, Rwanda, Samoa, Samoa (American), Scotland, Senegal, Serbia, Sierra Leone, Singapore, South Africa, Spain, Sri Lanka, St. Kitts, St. Lucia, St. Maartan, St. Vincent, Sudan, Suriname, Sweden, Switzerland, Tajikistan, Tanzania, Thailand, Togo, Tonga, Trinidad/ Tobago, Turks & Caicos Islands, Uganda, Ukraine, United States, Uruguay, Uzbekistan, Venezuela, Vietnam, Virgin Islands (American), Virgin Islands (British), Wales, Yugoslavia, Zambia, Zimbabwe, and other nations.

To find your nearest Aglow Fellowship, call or write us at:

P.O. Box 1749, Edmonds, WA 98020-1749
Phone: 425-775-7282 or 1-800-793-8126
Fax: 425-778-9615 / Email: aglow@aglow.org
Website: http://www.aglow.org/